P9-CSE-336

Salvador DALÍ

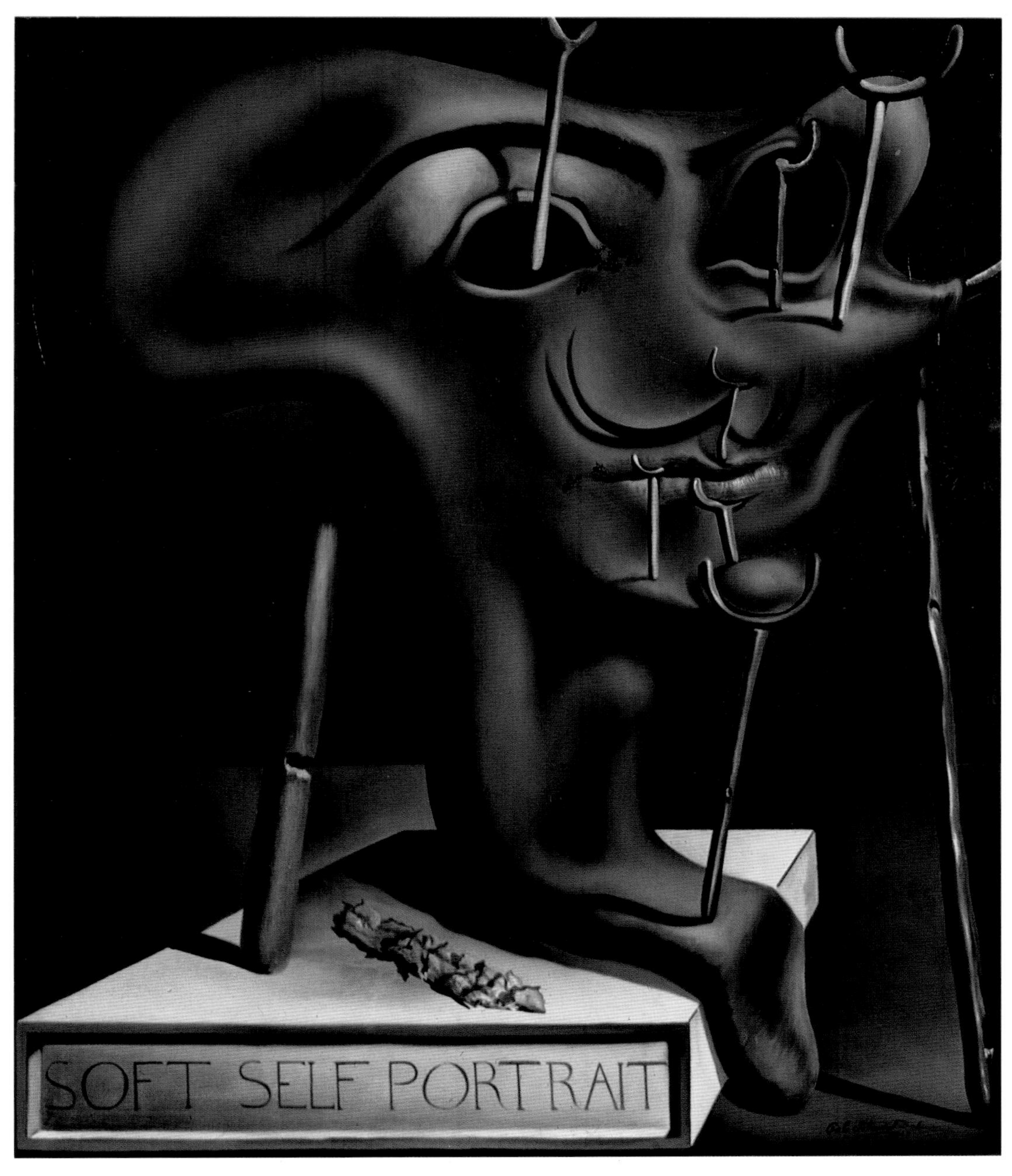

Salvador DALÍ

JESSICA HODGE

This edition published by
Barnes & Noble, Inc.,
by arrangement with Brompton
Books Corporation

Produced by Brompton Books
Corporation
15 Sherwood Place
Greenwich, CT 06830

ISBN 1-56619-180-7

Printed in Spain

PAGE 1: Dalí's *Soft Self-Portrait with a Rasher of Grilled Bacon, 1941.*

PAGE 2: *The Metamorphosis of Narcissus* (detail), 1937.

BELOW: *Apparition of Face and Fruit Dish on a Beach*, 1938.

CONTENTS

INTRODUCTION

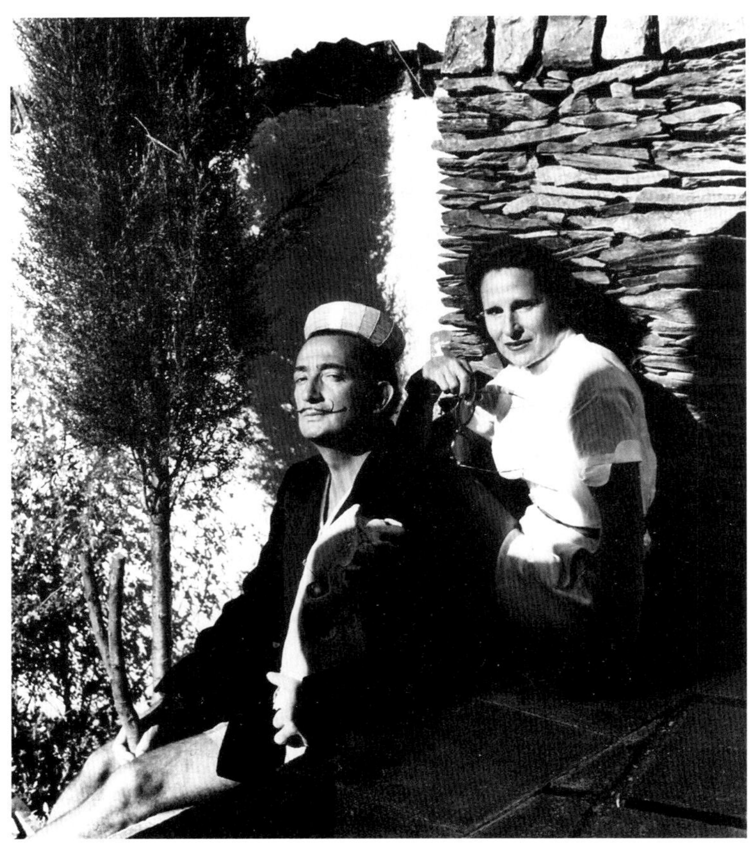

During the years of his decline, and particularly after the death of his beloved wife and inseparable companion Gala in 1982, Salvador Dalí was remembered more for his eccentricities and conjuring tricks than for his painting. His most prolonged and inspired period of creativity was in the 1920s and 1930s when, under the influence of Surrealism, he painted many of his best-known and most original works. Later in his career he seemed more concerned with living the life of a celebrity and cultivating his reputation for outrageousness than with furthering his art. Stories of his self-publicity are legion. On his first arrival in New York in 1934, he approached waiting journalists waving an eight-foot-long stick of bread that the ship's baker had specially prepared for him. When invited to do a window dressing for the Bonwit Teller store on New York's Fifth Avenue, he flew into a rage with a store employee who moved his arrangement of bathtub and mannequin, and in the resulting fracas he and the tub crashed through the window into the street. He once arrived at the Sorbonne in a Rolls-Royce full of cauliflowers; undertook a whole lecture tour dressed in a diving suit; and appeared wearing a tuxedo adorned with imitation flies.

Many serious commentators dismissed him altogether in his later years as nothing but a showman, and this assessment seemed to be confirmed by his bizarre decline and death. In 1974, customs officials seized some 40,000 sheets of paper bearing Dalí's signature; apparently these were to have been used for supposedly limited runs of prints. Dalí's assistants maintained that he had signed them all, while Dalí claimed that he had been betrayed by his entourage. Two years after Gala's death he emerged from self-imposed seclusion after being badly burnt when his bed caught fire. He weighed a mere 100 pounds, was suffering from severe malnutrition, and was convinced that he could neither stand nor swallow. He recovered, however, and retired to an isolated existence in his childhood home of Figueras, in the province of Catalonia in north-east Spain, finally dying on 23 January 1989.

He had been born in Figueras 85 years earlier, the second Salvador Dalí y Domenech of his generation. Shortly before his birth, his parents had lost their first-born son, also named Salvador, and they doted on their abnormally sensitive and excitable second son with an overprotective love that reinforced his already self-absorbed nature. Dalí's father was a lawyer and a republican, a notable local figure in Figueras; his mother, with whom he retained a close and loving relationship throughout her life, was a devout Catholic. Dalí's childhood and his adolescent experiences remained a primary motivating force throughout his career. He maintained that he could remember his own birth, describing it as a 'horrible traumatism,' and events from his early years, whether real, embroidered or wholly imaginary, informed some of his works' most persistent images.

As a child Dalí displayed a craving for solitude, interspersed with outbreaks of attention-seeking and exhibitionism. He would spend hours sitting in a water-filled washtub in the laundry room at the top of the family house, absorbed in the workings of his own imagination. After a year at the state school in Figueras, his father despaired of his learning anything and moved him, at the age of eight, to a local private school. From this period stem three images that recur frequently in his art: two cypress trees, visible through the classroom window; a reproduction of Jean-François Millet's *The*

LEFT: Salvador and Gala Dalí at Port Lligat. In 1930 Dalí bought a small fisherman's cottage in this village near Cadaqués, and continued to use it periodically for the rest of his life.

RIGHT: Dalí pictured during his lengthy stay, 1940-48, in the United States. His departure from the European scene marked the final break with André Breton, leader of the Surrealist movement, but in the U.S. he was hailed as a media personality. In 1941 the Museum of Modern Art, New York, held a retrospective exhibition of his work, which in turn led to a number of celebrity portrait commissions.

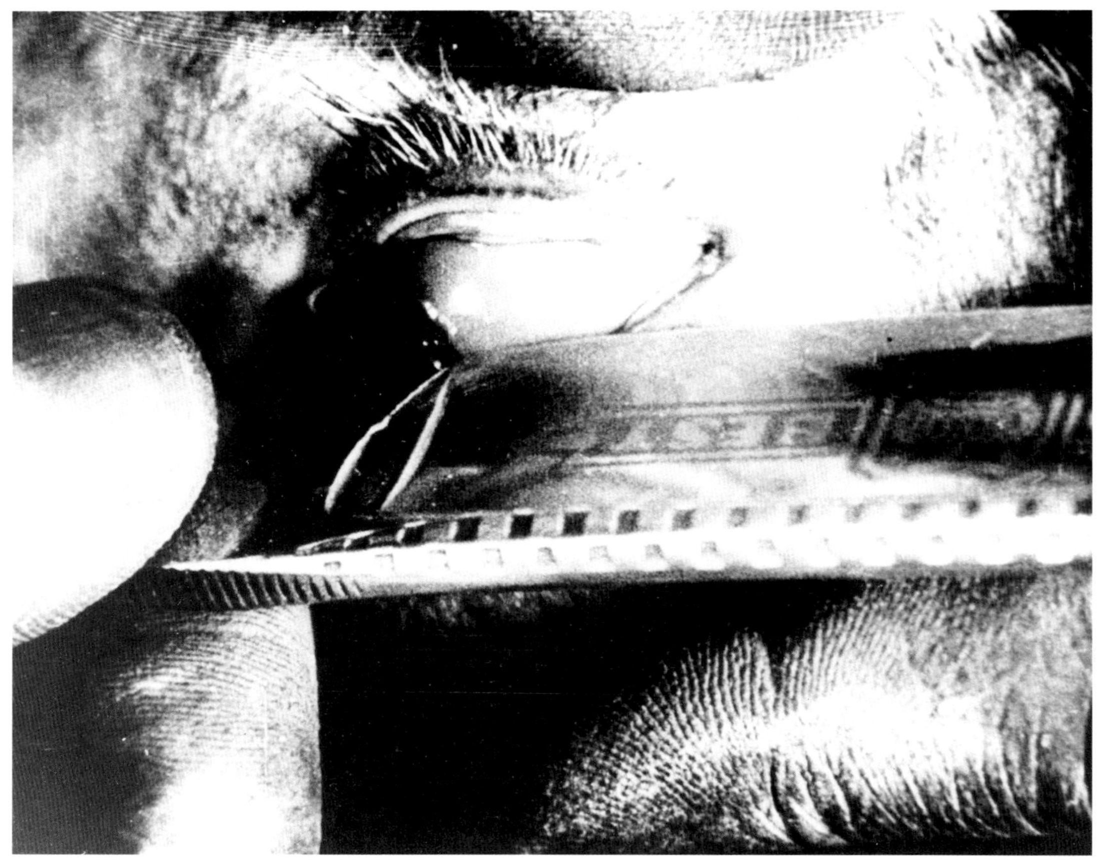

LEFT: In 1929 Dalí joined Luis Buñuel in Paris for the shooting of the film *Un Chien Andalou*, on the script of which they had worked together the previous winter. Buñuel wrote of this: 'In the working out of the plot, every idea of a rational, aesthetic, or other preoccupation with technical matters, was rejected as irrelevant. The result is a film deliberately anti-plastic, anti-artistic.' This notorious shot comes from the opening sequence: Buñuel himself is shown testing a razor blade on his thumb before the slitting of a girl's eye, for which they used an ox's eye.

RIGHT: Dalí pays extravagant homage to Gala at their home in Port Lligat. They first met in the summer of 1929, when Gala accompanied her husband, the Surrealist poet Paul Eluard, on a visit to Dalí in Figueras. Dalí had embarked on a period of intense creativity, during which he produced some of his most quintessentially Surrealist works, but was also in a hysterical state verging on madness. Gala became a source of both inspiration and relative equanimity for him, and they soon became inseparable companions.

RIGHT: This photograph of the Surrealist group taken in 1929/30 shows Dalí seated second left with, among others, Paul Eluard, Max Ernst, Man Ray, and André Breton.

Angelus; and a figure of Christ on the cross whose feet the children touched as they crossed themselves on leaving school.

The young and precocious Dalí expressed an early enthusiasm for painting and drawing. He spent hours poring over the art books which his father gave him, and made his first oil paintings at the age of eight. Soon afterward he was sent by his parents to stay with their friends the Pitchots, a cultured and musically gifted family with a country home not far from Figueras. Here he was fascinated by the work of the Impressionist painter Ramón Pitchot, who had worked with Picasso during the summer of 1911 in the nearby fishing village of Cadaqués. Inspired to create his own masterpiece, Dalí painted a still life of cherries on a worm-eaten door, using only three colors and squeezing the oils direct from the tube. When challenged that his cherries had no stalks, he glued the stalks of the real cherries that he had

RIGHT: A feast of sea urchins for Dalí and Gala.

RIGHT: Just before the outbreak of World War II, Dalí was in New York working on a monumental set piece for the 1939 New York World's Fair. Called the *Dream of Venus*, this was to consist of a giant water tank filled with real and model sirens and various other objects, with a Surrealist landscape backcloth, and huge reproductions of the *Mona Lisa* and Botticelli's *Birth of Venus*. Some of Dalí's more bizarre ideas provoked resistance among the promoters, however, and the final installation was a compromise.

been using as a model onto the painted fruit, then laboriously picked the woodworms out of the door using a hairpin, and transferred them to the hole in the cherries left by the stalks. The Pitchots were impressed, and it was at Ramón's suggestion that, at the age of 12, Dalí was enrolled in a local drawing class. A naturally gifted draftsman, he here acquired the academic skills and technique that were to remain one of the most consistent and characteristic qualities of his painting.

In his early teens Dalí painted constantly. The local landscape, which was to continue to feature in his mature work, was a regular subject, as were scenes of Spanish domestic life, and he also copied the works of established painters. Aged about 15, he and a group of friends produced a review called *Studium*, containing a section by Dalí on 'The Great Masters of Painting,' in which he first expressed his admiration for Velázquez, as well as writing on Goya, El Greco, Dürer, Leonardo and Michelangelo.

In September 1921 Dalí enrolled at the School of Fine Arts in Madrid. Already familiar with Impressionism, he began to experiment here with the most avant-garde styles, including Fauvism, Cubism, Futurism, with its rejection of all art of the past, and Purism, with its emphasis on clarity, functionalism and objectivity. One of the earliest paintings to reflect Dalí's move away from the Impressionist style that had so far characterized his work is *Self-Portrait with the Neck of Raphael*, 1921. Taking as its background the Costa Brava coast around the fishing village of Cadaqués, where he spent his childhood summers, this shows Dalí's adoption of the exuberant colors and divisionist technique of Fauvist painters such as Matisse and Derain. This style in turn soon gave way to such Cubist-inspired works as *Cubist Self-Portrait* (1922-23) while, at the same time, Dalí continued to paint in a more traditional realistic mode. This simultaneous playing with radically different styles makes the paintings of the early 1920s difficult to date.

Dalí found the teaching at the Madrid academy tedious and outdated, however, and continued to cultivate his reputation for eccentricity. When asked to draw a statue of the Virgin from a model, he gave his appalled teacher a drawing of a pair of scales. He wore outlandish clothes, strolling the streets of Madrid in short pants, a black felt cap and an ankle-length cape. After a period of introspective isolation, he became absorbed into an avant-garde student group which included the future film-maker Luis Buñuel and the Andalusian poet Federico García Lorca. He also became identified by the academy authorities as a rebel, and in October 1923 was suspended for a year, accused of insubordination. On his return in 1924 he abandoned the self-conscious bohemianism of his earlier student days and adopted what was to become the more familiar role of dandy, brilliantining his hair, dressing fastidiously and expensively, and developing a taste for cocktails. His Madrid lifestyle was in marked contrast to the extreme asceticism of the summers spent in Figueras or Cadaqués, but in all these places his artistic output was prodigious. The poet Rafael Alberti, another member of the radical student group, later recalled:

> Dalí had a formidable vocation and . . . was an astonishing draftsman. He drew as he wished, from nature or from his imagination. His line was classical and pure. His perfect stroke, which recalled the Picasso of the hellenistic period, was no less admirable.

In 1925 Dalí had his first one-man exhibition, at the Dalmau Gallery in Barcelona. This included works in a classical style as well as Cubist and Purist paintings. Despite this stylistic incoherence it was a critical success; one reviewer hailed the artist as greatly gifted, singling out the realist *Girl Standing at the Window* for particular praise. Perhaps more importantly, the show was seen and admired by both Miró and Picasso. When Dalí made his first trip to Paris the following spring, he visited Picasso and was given a private tour of the artist's studio. Given the range and sophistication of Dalí's references and contacts, it is perhaps not surprising that he was less than co-operative during his final examination at the Madrid academy that summer: when asked to choose a subject, he withdrew from one exam on the basis that none of the supervisors was competent to judge him. This, combined with other breaches of discipline, led to his expulsion, but Dalí was already hard at work on the preparations for his next one-man show. His career was launched.

The second show, again at the Dalmau Gallery, provoked a more mixed critical response. Picasso's influence was even more evident in what Dalí described

RIGHT: During his stay in the United States, Dalí painted a number of society portraits, including this one dating from 1948, which provoked criticism in the art world that he was compromising his artistic integrity.

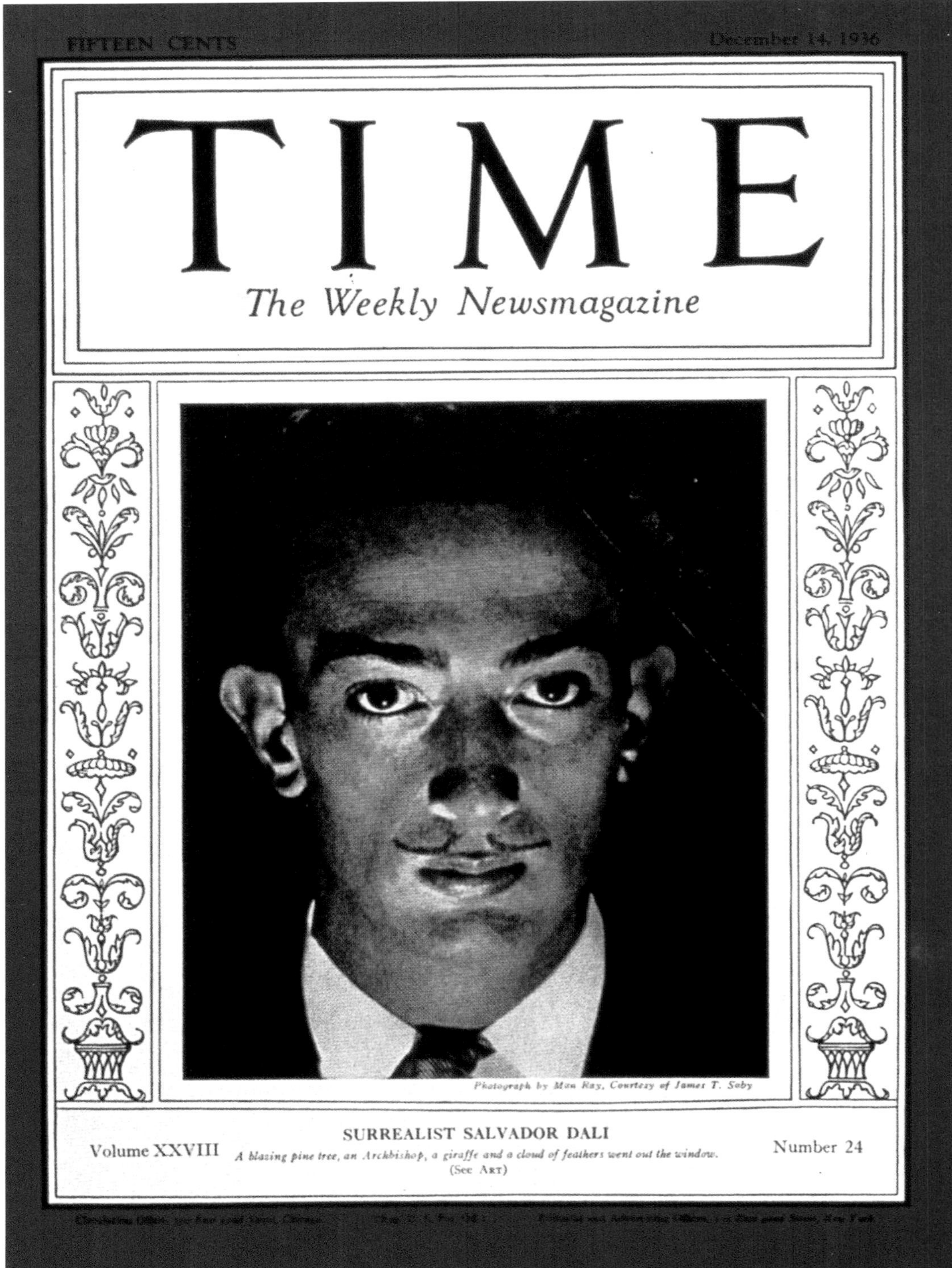

FIFTEEN CENTS
December 14, 1936
TIME
The Weekly Newsmagazine
Photograph by Man Ray, Courtesy of James T. Soby
Volume XXVIII
SURREALIST SALVADOR DALI
A blazing pine tree, an Archbishop, a giraffe and a cloud of feathers went out the window.
(See ART)
Number 24

LEFT: By 1936 Dalí was a sufficiently international figure for *Time* magazine to feature this 1933 photograph by Man Ray on its cover. It was partly his very success that led to the break with the Surrealists.

RIGHT: Dalí's early painting style, before his studies in Madrid introduced him to the Catalan avant-garde, was influenced by the Impressionists. In his teens he spent several summers in the fishing village of Cadaqués, producing a number of landscapes, including this view of *The Bay at Cadaqués*.

as his 'neo-Cubist' works, such as *Femme Couchée*. Here he returned to a subject which he had already explored in *Bathers of the Costa Brava* (1921) and which continued to fascinate him: the sun-worshippers who gathered to disport themselves on the Costa Brava beaches. Subject is all that the paintings have in common, however: while the earlier one is diffuse and atmospheric, *Femme Couchée* has a massive sculptural quality reminiscent of Picasso's classical style and, with its overt, depersonalized sexuality, introduces a theme that came increasingly to dominate Dalí's work in the late 1920s.

Dalí's relationships with Buñuel and Lorca continued to play a major role in his development as an artist after they had left Madrid. In 1925 and 1926, Lorca was a frequent visitor at the Dalí family home in Figueras. Together Lorca and Dalí made contact with the Catalan avant-garde, and Lorca arranged a production of his first lyrical drama, *Mariana Pineda*, in Barcelona in 1927, with scenery designed by Dalí. It was to Lorca that Dalí wrote in autumn 1927 with news of the most radical departure in his painting so far, which hints at the Surrealist works to come:

Federico, I am painting pictures which make me die for joy. I am creating with an absolute naturalness, without the slightest aesthetic concern, I am making things which inspire me with a very profound emotion . . . At the moment I am painting a very

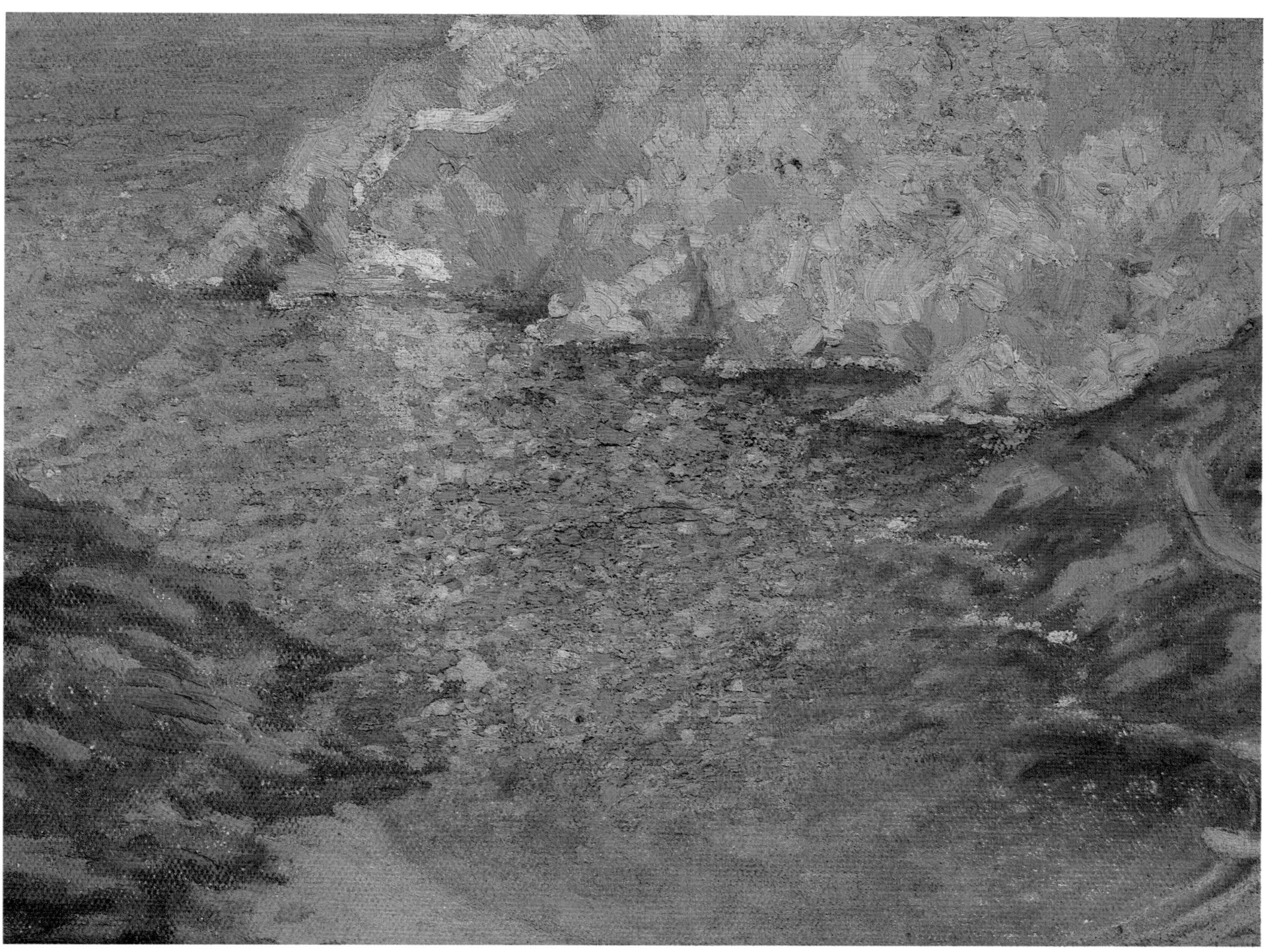

beautiful woman, smiling, tickled by multicolored feathers, supported by a little burning marble die, the side of the marble in turn is held up by a tiny plume of smoke, which trails peacefully, in the sky there are clouds with little parrots' heads, and sand from the beach.

It was probably through the Catalan artistic and literary avant-garde that Dalí made his first contact with Surrealism. This, initially primarily a literary movement, developed in Paris in the 1920s as a direct descendant of the anti-war movement Dada, with its commitment to the destruction of all existing values in life and art. Surrealism condemned the existing 'classical' tradition – the idea of truth to nature and art for its own sake – but also rejected the nihilism of Dada by seeking to identify an alternative tradition in the work of painters of fantasy such as Bosch and Uccello, Symbolist art and writings, and naïve and primitive art. Proponents of the movement maintained that the surreal had always been an integral, if undervalued, part of human consciousness. The aim of Surrealism was to plumb the human psyche for artistic inspiration, and Freud's *The Interpretation of Dreams* was a critical influence in its early development.

In 1924 André Breton, the main architect of Surrealism, gave the classic definition of the movement in the *Surrealist Manifesto*, describing it as:

Pure psychic automatism, by which one proposes to express . . . the actual functioning of thought. Dictated by thought, in the absence of any control exercised by reason, exempt from any aesthetic or moral concern . . . Surrealism is based on the belief in the superiority of certain forms of previously neglected associations, in the omnipotence of dreams, in the disinterested play of thought.

Only by allowing the unconscious full play, according to Breton, could the Surrealist image occur spontaneously, its full beauty revealed in the juxtaposition of dream and reality. By inducing trance-states, the Surrealists found that they could tap a world of heightened reality, a hitherto repressed psychic life. The aim of Surrealism became 'the future resolution of these two states, dream and reality, which are seemingly so contradictory, into a kind of absolute reality, a *surreality*.'

In 1927 nine months' compulsory military service forced Dalí to abandon painting for a while, but this hiatus seems to have given him the opportunity to take

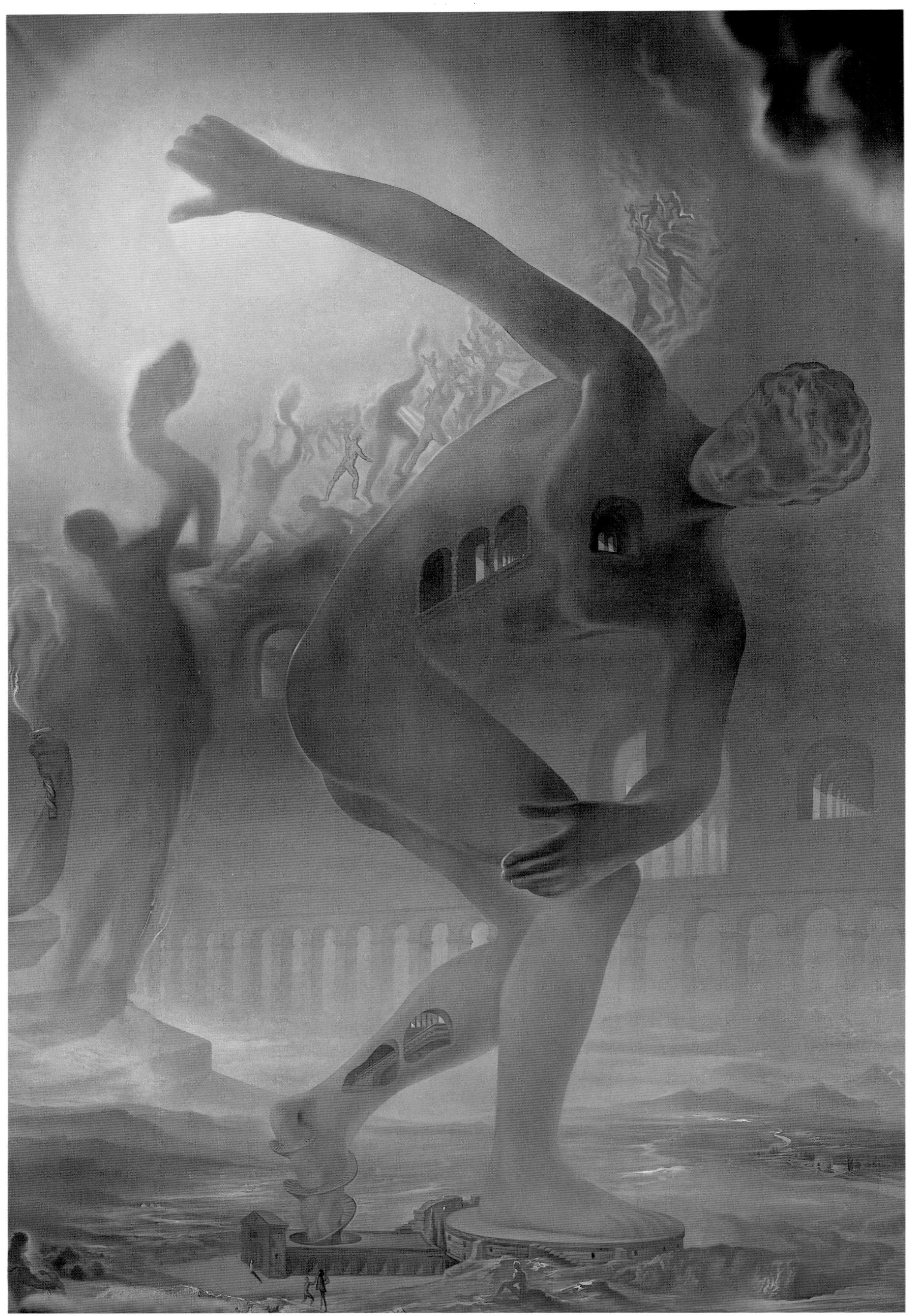

LEFT: *The Cosmic Athlete* reflects Dalí's synthesis in the 1950s and 1960s of the classical preoccupations of Renaissance art with the principles of physics and metaphysics then being formulated.

RIGHT: *The Angelus*, 1857-59, by Jean-François Millet. A reproduction of this painting hung on the wall of the school to which Dalí was sent at the age of eight, and was to prove an endless source of inspiration for him.

stock of his artistic future. His ecstatic letter to Lorca indicates the direction this was to take. One of the first works he painted at the end of 1927 was *Apparatus and Hand*, which both demonstrates Dalí's assimilation of the Surrealist ethos of dream imagery, and introduces the theme of masturbation, symbolized by the swollen, veined hand surmounting the apparatus, which was to preoccupy him for the next five years.

At this stage, Dalí's knowledge of Surrealism was gleaned from review articles and discussions rather than from direct contact with Surrealist work. His own painting remained extremely varied and eclectic in style, combining Surrealist elements, such as the soft amorphous shapes of *The Bather* (1928), with well-established themes such as the sunbathers of Cadaqués. He seemed to feel a temporary sense of dissatisfaction

RIGHT: In 1984 Dalí was rescued from a fire at the medieval castle of Pubol into which he had retired after Gala's death in 1982. The world was shocked at his appearance: he believed himself unable either to stand or to swallow and was suffering from severe malnutrition, weighing only 100 pounds.

with painting as a medium for the expression of the ideas that were beginning to preoccupy him. This can be discerned in his emphasis at this time on the objective vision to be achieved by film and photography, in preference to painting, as revealing the potential fantasy in objects themselves. In December 1927 he dedicated to Buñuel an article on the art of film, and the following year the two friends collaborated on what Buñuel described as 'a formidable scenario, with no precedent in the history of cinema.' This was *Un Chien Andalou*, the film which was to make Dalí's reputation, with its savage confrontation between the rational and irrational. The rapid montage sequences in the film achieve exactly that effect of a dream rooted in an objective world which Dalí was exploring in his writings, but not fully in his art. Nonetheless, some of the film images, such as the putrefying donkey, the swarming ants, the enlarged hand, relate to the obsessional themes of eroticism, death and decay that had already made their appearance in his painting.

At the end of 1928 Dalí again visited Paris to work with Buñuel on the shooting of *Un Chien Andalou*. His fellow Catalan, Joan Miró, at that time a leading Surrealist painter, acted as his guide and introduced him to the Surrealist group, yet the main impression from Dalí's own writings of this time is of isolation and loss of direction. The Surrealist group was racked by dissension and defections, and Dalí remained on the fringes only, despite the rapturous reception accorded to his first truly Surrealist work, *The First Days of Spring*. He returned to Figueras in the summer of 1929 in a state of nervous exhaustion, a prey to delirious fantasies and hysterical laughter.

Dalí's outstanding contribution to the Surrealist movement, which gave his own work a new cogency and clarification, was his development of what he later defined as the 'paranoiac-critical method.' In his autobiography, *The Secret Life of Salvador Dalí* (1942), he described how he would trace a succession of images in the stains on his school's classroom ceiling, then discovering that he could recall these images at will. This conscious element in the accessing of the subconscious was expounded by Dalí in various writings between 1929 and 1935, and was hailed by André Breton as 'an instrument of primary importance.'

On his return to Figueras, Dalí at once began work on *The Lugubrious Game*, the first of a major group of paintings dating from 1929. The central characteristic of these is their conscious use of the vocabulary of psychoanalysis, culled from the psychology textbooks

LEFT: Dalí and Gala pictured in London in 1951 in front of *The Madonna of Port Lligat* (1949) (see page 107). Gala regularly served as his model; here she is depicted as the Madonna in a painting modeled on Piero della Francesca's altarpiece *Madonna and Child with Saints* (1492-94). The ostrich egg suspended over the Virgin's head is a medieval symbol of the Virgin Birth, but the elements of the painting are suspended in space like particles of atomic matter, reflecting Dalí's harnessing of the discoveries of nuclear physics to religious subject matter.

RIGHT: A young and romantic Dalí in contemplative mood in Connecticut, 1939.

LEFT: In 1922-23 Dalí experimented with pointillism, the technique of painting with dots of color pioneered by Georges Seurat. *Bathers of the Costa Brava* (1923) also illustrates his obsession with the sun-worshipping hedonists on the Figueras beaches.

RIGHT: The British actor Laurence Olivier, in one of his most famous film roles as Shakespeare's Richard III, poses for Dalí in 1955.

BELOW: The preparatory drawing for Dalí's *Bullfighter* displays both his faultless draftsmanship and the restless energy that drove him.

which Dalí had been studying, combined with deeply personal, autobiographical references to his own neurotic fear and sexual anxiety, his obsession with masturbation and the sense of guilt that this provoked.

In the course of the summer Dalí was visited by some of the members of the Surrealist group whom he had met in Paris: the Belgian painter René Magritte and his wife, the Paris art dealer Camille Goemans, and the poet Paul

Eluard and his wife Gala. They were fascinated both by Dalí's work and by his unusual personality, but were concerned that the scatological elements in *The Lugubrious Game* might reflect an abnormal psychological state rather than a Surrealist expression of uncensored thought. Gala was deputed to question Dalí, and he assured her that 'I consider scatology as a terrorizing element, just as I do blood, or my phobia of grasshoppers.' This satisfied the group as to Dalí's Surrealist credentials, and from that time he was admitted to the heart of the movement.

As a further result of this momentous visit, Gala, who at first found Dalí bizarre and repellent, became intrigued by his manic personality, and found that she had the power to bring him relief from the demonic images that were tormenting him. Although they only married in 1958, she became his muse and the object of his intense devotion from that time, staying with him for a while in the summer of 1929 after the rest of the group had left. During this time Dalí gradually conquered his hysteria, and when she too left he threw himself into his work and painted two of his most significant pictures, *The Enigma of Desire* and *The Great Masturbator*. These established his reputation with the Surrealists and also had the effect of reinvigorating the movement; their minute detailing and obsessive sexual content, combined with their masterly academic technique, epitomized the Surrealist mission, defined by Breton as 'the perpetual excursion into the midst of the forbidden zone.'

One of the earliest manifestations of the paranoiac-critical method that Dalí explored took the form of a chain of irrational objects arising out of a single image. *The Lugubrious Game*, in which a crowd of images – a grasshopper, a rabbit's head, Dalí's own face – spiral out of a truncated body, is one of the first examples of this, and in the early 1930s Dalí applied this chain of irrational association both to the legend of William Tell, and to Millet's painting of *The Angelus*. The William Tell

LEFT: Ever the showman, an ageing Dalí publicizes an exhibition of lithographs in 1971, supported by Gala, a couple of angelic children, goats – and the inevitable press pack.

RIGHT: Dalí returned to Spain in 1948 after eight years in America and, despite his internationalism, he continued to be absorbed and fascinated by his native country. This is his interpretation of that most Spanish of blood sports, *Bullfighter Killing the Bull*.

theme became bound up with the break that occurred at this time in Dalí's relationship with his father, partly as a result of his affair with Gala Eluard; he interpreted the story as signifying paternal threat, and therefore as a castration myth. *The Angelus* had fascinated him as a child, but he only now began to analyze this obsession. He identified Millet's pious couple, pausing in their labors in the field to pray as the church bell sounds, as representing a maternal variant on the myth of the father who devours his sons. The figures from *The Angelus* first appear in Dali's *Imperial Monument to the Child Woman* (*c.*1930), which also contains the *Mona Lisa* and a bust of Napoleon. From 1933 they feature constantly in his work.

As well as the chain of irrationally associated images explored in the works of the early and mid-1930s, Dalí also developed his theory of the double image. He described this as 'the image of an object which, without the least figurative or anatomical modification, can at the same time represent another, absolutely different, image.' Instead of being sequential, the hallucinatory images which the artist experiences as a result of his paranoiac-critical activity interrelate simultaneously. This was to prove by far the most fruitful application of the paranoiac-critical method, and is stated explicitly in the title of one painting: *Invisible Sleeping Woman, Horse, Lion* (1930). Here the triple image of the title seems to undergo a process of metamorphosis from sleeper to horse to lion. In later works Dalí mastered the technique of making two images interrelate completely, so that two consistent and independent alternative readings are possible.

The first wholly successful work of this type is *The Phantom Cart* (1933), a relatively simplified image in which a cart moving away from the viewer toward a distant town becomes driverless as the driver seems to be replaced by a tower seen through the cart's covering. By the mid-1930s Dalí was applying the double image to far

more complex works. In *Impressions of Africa* (1938) the double images cluster at the periphery of the painting, around a depiction of himself painting. By this time Dalí and Gala had left war-torn Spain and traveled to Italy, where he expressed the horror of civil war in the partial double imagery of *Spain* (1938), in which his homeland is shown as a woman whose head and upper torso can be read as a group of fighting and fleeing figures, and her breasts as picadors who have turned their lances on each other.

Dalí continued to work spasmodically with the double image throughout his life – *The Hallucinogenic*

LEFT: Dalí with his *Christ of St. John of the Cross* when it was exhibited in London in 1951. Here he recreates the style of the Spanish painter Francisco de Zurbarán (1598-1644), based on a drawing made by the Spanish mystic St. John of the Cross, which broke with traditional images of the Crucifixion by showing it from above. Dalí used a Hollywood stuntman to make preliminary studies from life for his version, which has become one of his most famous works, although coolly received at the time.

Toreador (1968-70) is a late example – but he never again achieved the burst of creativity of the late 1930s. Toward the end of the decade he painted a number of pictures which, while showing an increasing technical sophistication, also suggest a decline in hallucinatory force. Breton said of works such as *Apparition of Face and Fruit Dish on Beach* (1938), and *The Endless Enigma* (1938) that:

> By wanting to be punctilious in his paranoiac method, it can be observed that he is beginning to fall prey to a diversion of the order of a crossword puzzle.

A further cause of distancing between Dalí and the Surrealists was that, for them, the exploration of the irrational was only ever intended to be a preliminary to the final unification of the personality, the 'future resolution of these two states, dream and reality.' For Dalí, on the other hand, the irrational was an end in itself: he wanted to 'systematize confusion and contribute to the total discrediting of the world of reality.' This difference combined with Dalí's increasingly right-wing political stance – his support for General Franco was partly a reaction to his father's republicanism – to cause a breach with Breton and the Surrealists. This was irrevocably finalized when, on arrival in New York in 1940, Dalí declared: 'I am Surrealism.'

In the U.S.A. Dalí's painting output slowed, although he continued to produce the occasional archetypal Surrealist work, as in the dream transcription and interpretation of *One Second Before Awakening From a Dream Caused by the Flight of a Bee Around a Pomegranate* (1944). Instead he threw himself into the social and commercial whirlpool of American life, resolved to become 'the greatest courtesan' of his time. For eight years he and Gala divided their time between California and New York, and Dalí designed jewelry, painted society portraits, collaborated with Schiaparelli on a new perfume, wrote his autobiography and a novel, and worked with Alfred Hitchcock on a dream sequence for the film *Spellbound*. He amassed a considerable fortune, inspiring

RIGHT: *The Battle of Tetuan* (1962) was exhibited in Barcelona together with the nineteenth-century Spanish painter Fortuny's version of the same subject.

BELOW: *Woman in the Form of a Guitar* is a straightforward and explicit example of Dalí's theory of the double image.

Breton's bitter anagram on his name – Avida Dollars – but seemed directionless and expressed in his autobiography, published in 1942, a sense of spiritual aridity.

In 1945, however, the horror of Hiroshima and Nagasaki gave him a new focus. The scale and ferocity of such destruction suggested that the irrational now lay in the world of observed reality, rather than in his own mind. Declaring that 'after the First World War it was psychology; after the Second World War it shall be physics,' Dalí entered a new period of creative activity,

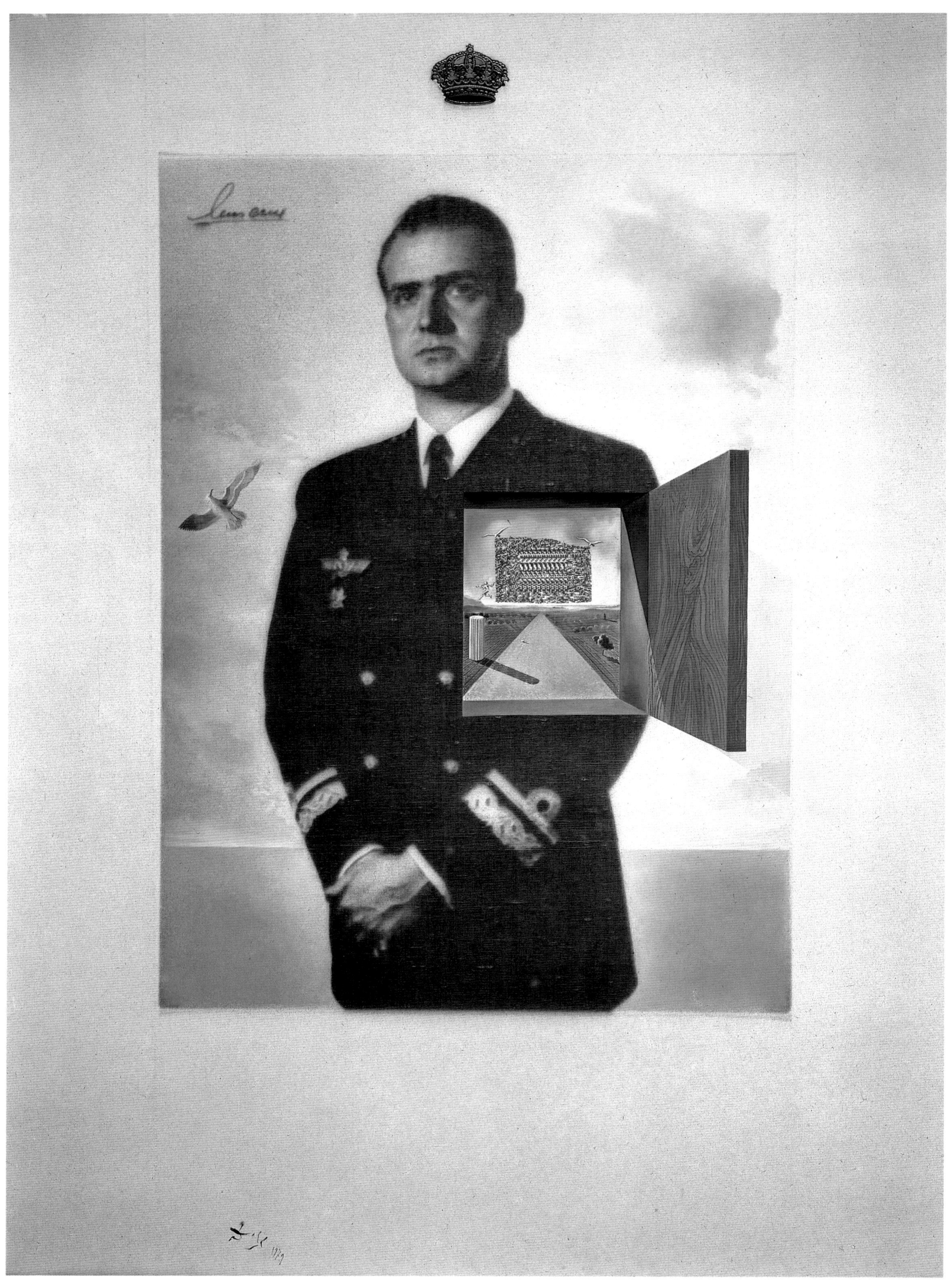

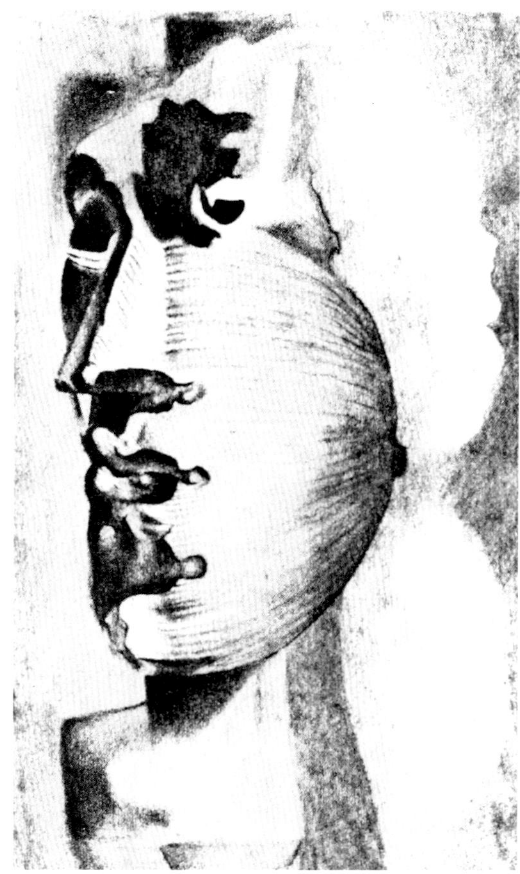

LEFT: *Portrait of King Juan Carlos*; after the death in 1975 of General Franco, leader of the rebel forces in the Spanish Civil War and head of state from 1939, Juan Carlos, grandson of King Alfonso XIII and Franco's chosen successor, became king.

RIGHT: *Paranoiac Face*, published in *Le Surréalisme au Service de la Révolution*, December 1931, the third of a series of major Surrealist reviews. An early use of the double image, this photograph of native Africans was identified as a Picasso-style face by Dalí as he shuffled through a pile of papers.

which he called 'nuclear painting.' In this he explored the discoveries of atomic physics concerning the structure of matter and, above all, the release of energy involved in the breaking of atomic particles. A sense of the divisibility of matter reappears constantly in the paintings of the later 1940s and 1950s. In *Raphaelesque Head Exploding* (1951) he incorporated the classical tradition by linking a Raphael head of the Virgin with the interior of the Pantheon in Rome, and then shattered them into multiple parts. The mystical or metaphysical element in this work found expression particularly in his use of religious subject matter at this time. The dramatic angle of the cross in *Christ of St. John of the Cross* (1951) was inspired by a drawing by the Spanish mystic St. John of the Cross.

In his later years, more particularly after his return to Spain in 1955, Dalí continued to draw inspiration from the discoveries of science. In the late 1950s he was fascinated by optical theory; in the 1960s he linked his religious themes with the discovery of DNA; in the 1970s he experimented with holography and stereoscopy as a new means of expression.

While undoubtedly one of the most famous names in twentieth-century art, Dalí's status remains controversial. It is perhaps ironic, given his expulsion from the ranks of Surrealism and the large body of his subsequent work, that in the public mind he remains the Surrealist painter *par excellence*, an identification reinforced by his eccentric lifestyle and relentless talent for self-publicity.

ABOVE
Self-Portrait with the Neck of Raphael 1920-21
Oil on canvas, 21¼×22½ inches (60×57 cm)
Spanish State Patrimony

RIGHT
Portrait of a Girl in a Landscape 1924
Oil on canvas, 38×26 inches (92×65 cm)
Spanish State Patrimony

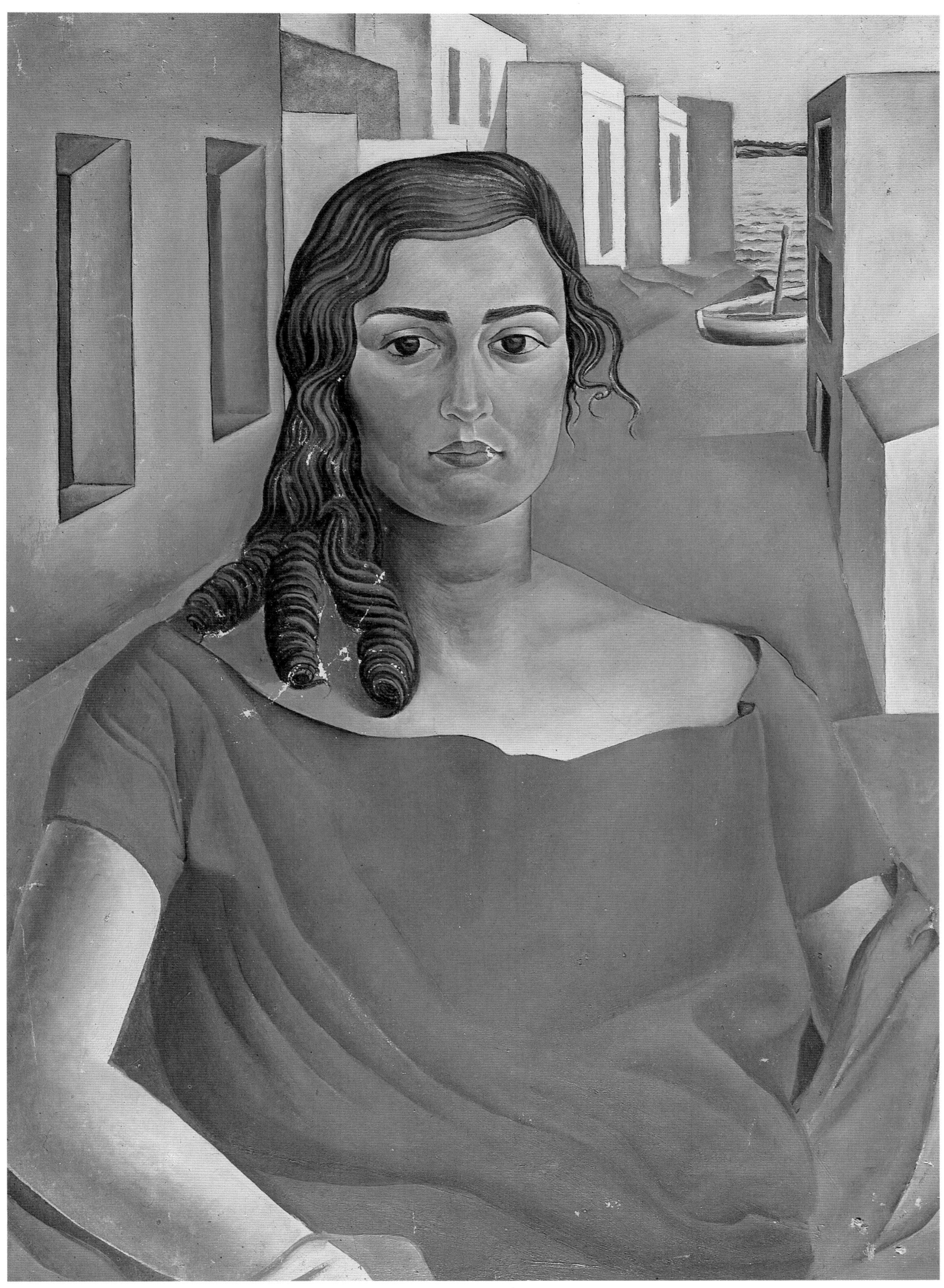

Portrait of Luis Buñuel 1924
Oil on canvas, 28×24 inches (70×60 cm)
Museo Español Arte Contemporáneo, Madrid

Portrait of the Artist's Father 1925
Oil on canvas, 49×33 inches (124.5×83.3 cm)
Private collection, Barcelona

Salvador Dalí
1925

ABOVE

Girl Standing at the Window 1925

Oil on canvas, 40½×29⅛ inches (101.3×73 cm)

Museo Arte Moderno, Madrid

LEFT

Seated Girl, Seen From the Back (The Artist's Sister) 1925

Oil on canvas, 42½×30¼ inches (108×76.8 cm)

Museo Español Arte Contemporáneo, Madrid

Femme Couchée 1926
Oil on panel, 10⅝×16 inches (27.3×40.6 cm)
Collection of The Salvador Dalí Museum, St. Petersburg, Florida

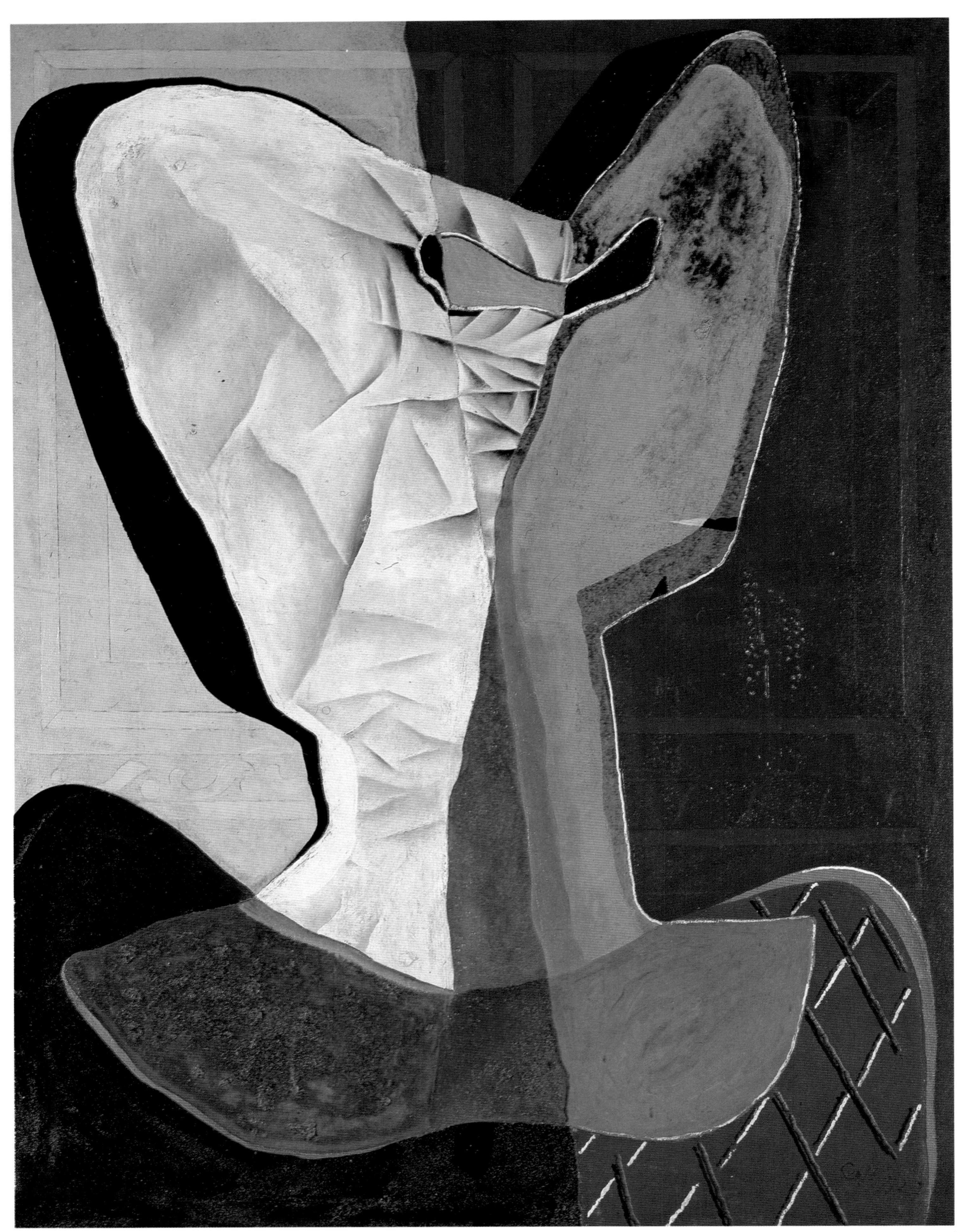

Harlequin 1927
Oil on canvas, 78×60 inches (195×150 cm)
Museo Español Arte Contemporáneo, Madrid

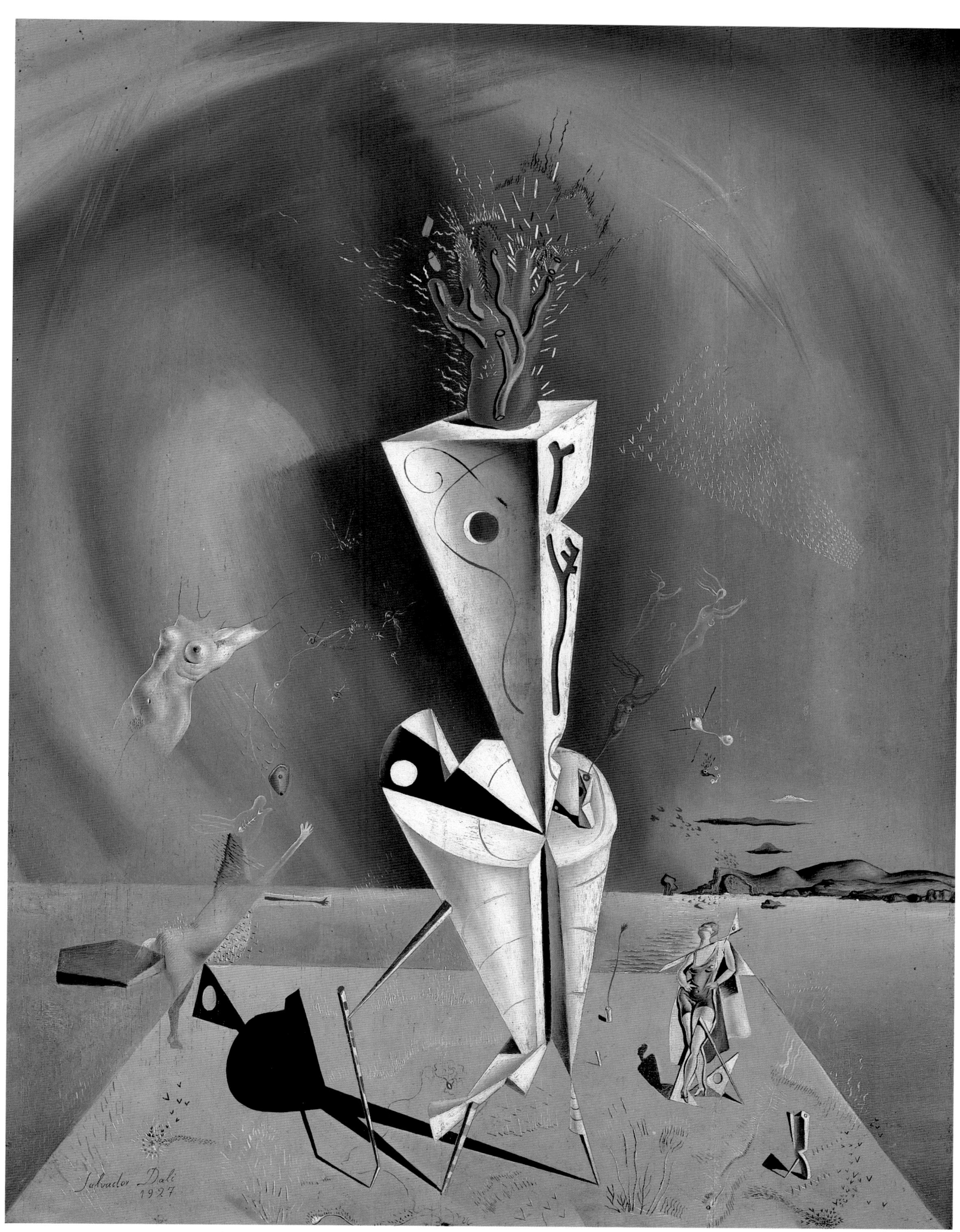

Apparatus and Hand 1927
Oil on panel, 24½×18¼ inches (62.2×46.3 cm)
Collection of Mr and Mrs A. Reynolds Morse,
on loan to The Salvador Dalí Museum, St. Petersburg, Florida

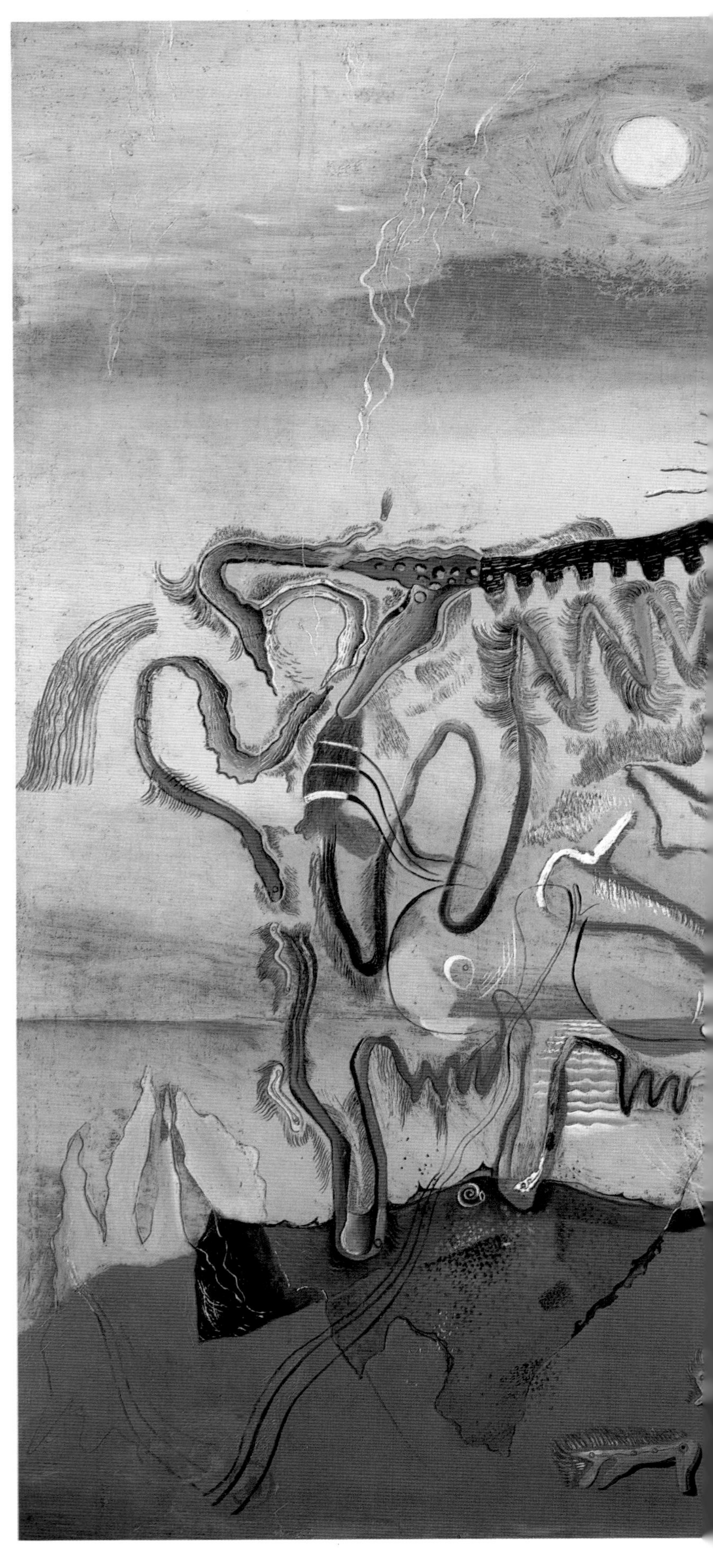

The Spectral Cow 1928
Oil on panel, 19⅝×25⅓ inches (50×64.5 cm)
Musée National d'Art Moderne, Centre Georges Pompidou, Paris

The Bather 1928
Oil on panel, 20½×28¼ inches (52×71.6 cm)
Collection of The Salvador Dalí Museum, St. Petersburg, Florida

salvador Dalí

The Enigma of Desire: My Mother, My Mother, My Mother 1929
Oil on canvas, 43⅝×59 inches (110.7×150 cm) Christie's, London

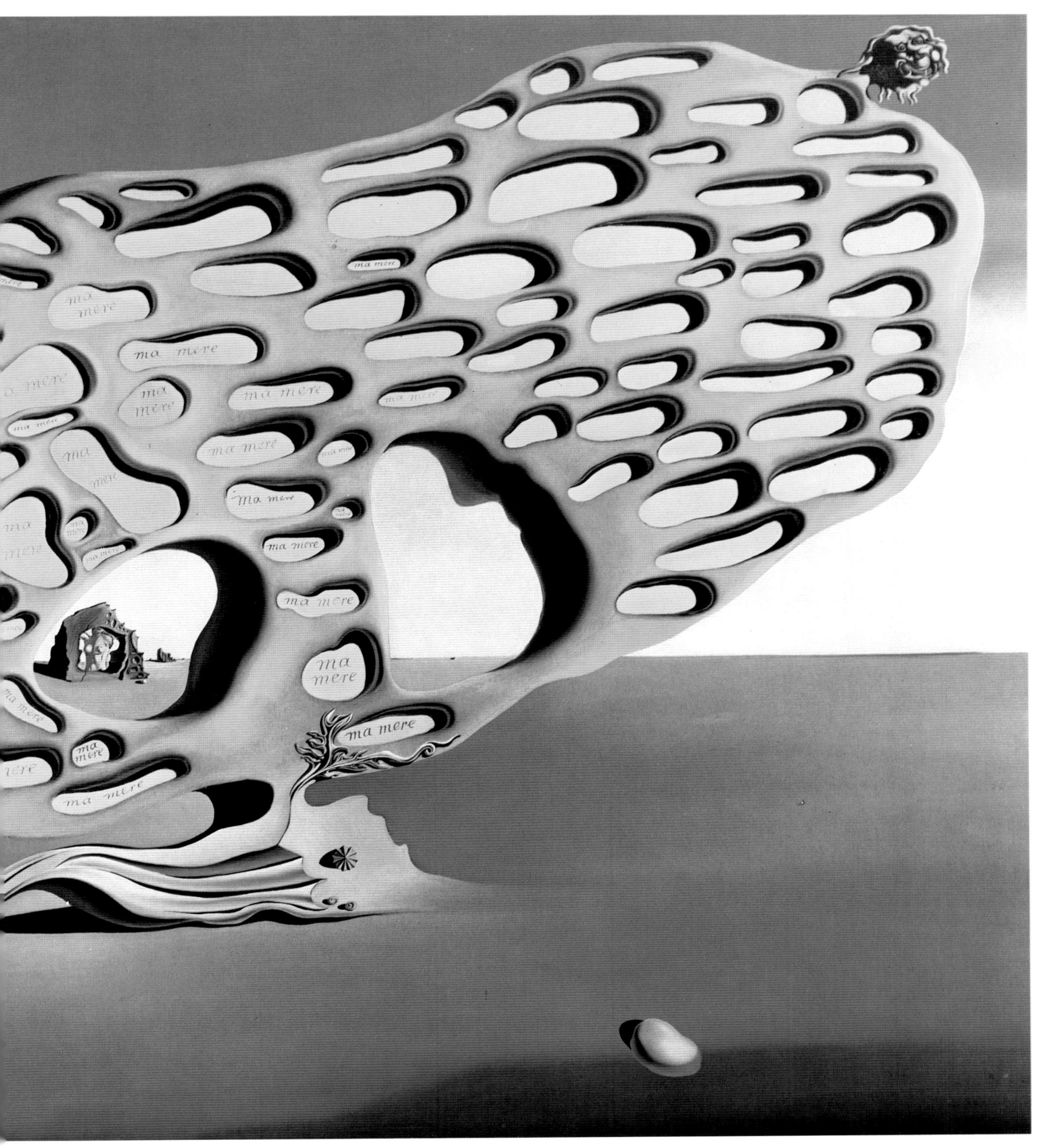
ma mere
ma mere
ma mere
ma mere
ma mere
ma mere
ma mere
ma mere
ma mere
ma mere
ma mere
ma mere
ma mere
ma mere
ma mere
ma mere

ABOVE
Cubist Self-Portrait *c.* 1922-23
Gouache and collage on cardboard, $41\frac{1}{4}\times29\frac{1}{4}$ inches (104.7×74.3 cm)
Spanish State Patrimony

LEFT
Imperial Monument to the Child Woman *c.*1930
Oil on canvas, $56\frac{7}{8}\times31\frac{7}{8}$ inches (142×81 cm)
Private collection, New York

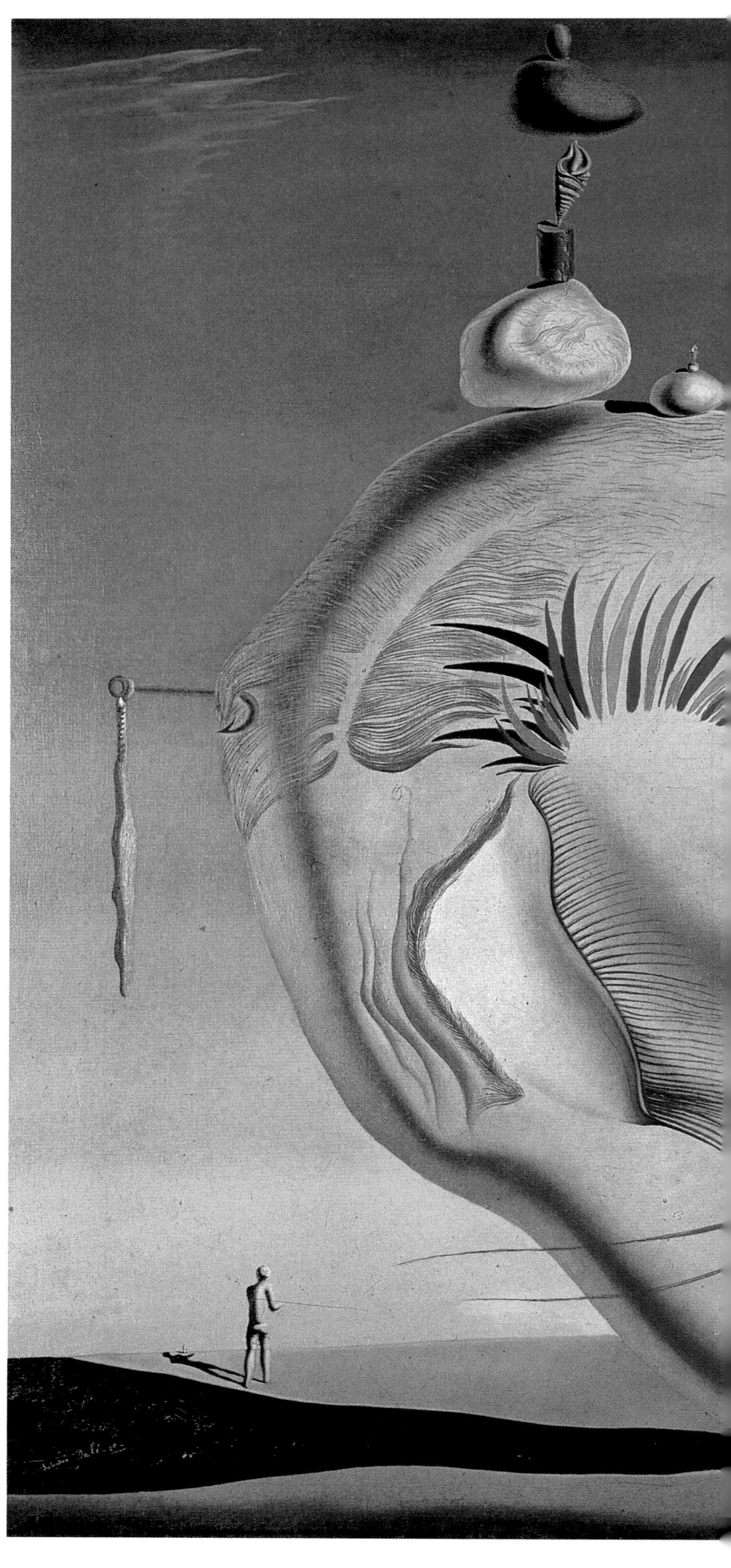

The Great Masturbator 1929
Oil on canvas, 44×46 inches (110×115 cm)
Spanish State Patrimony

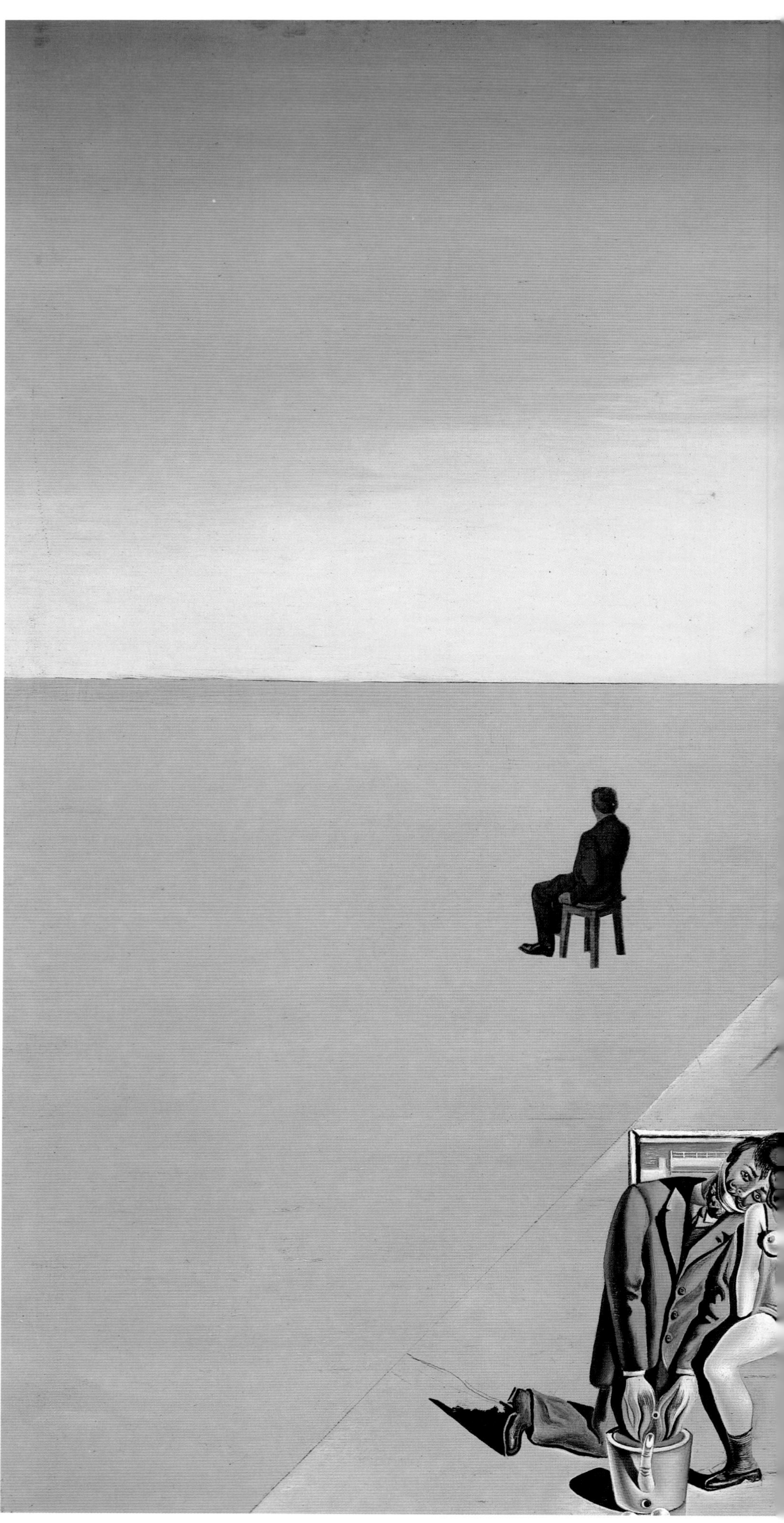

The First Days of Spring 1929
Oil on canvas, 19¾×24⅝ inches (49.4×61.5 cm)
Collection of Mr and Mrs A. Reynolds Morse, on loan to The Salvador Dalí Museum, St. Petersburg, Florida

Invisible Sleeping Woman, Horse, Lion 1930
Oil on canvas, 23⅝×27½ inches (60.7×70 cm)
Private collection

salvador Dalí 1930

La Main (Les Remords de Conscience) 1930
Oil on canvas, 16¼×26 inches (40.6×65 cm)
Collection of Mr and Mrs A. Reynolds Morse,
on loan to The Salvador Dalí Museum, St. Petersburg, Florida

The Birth of Liquid Desires 1931-32
Oil and collage on canvas, 38½×44⅞ inches (96.1×112.3 cm)
Peggy Guggenheim Collection, Venice

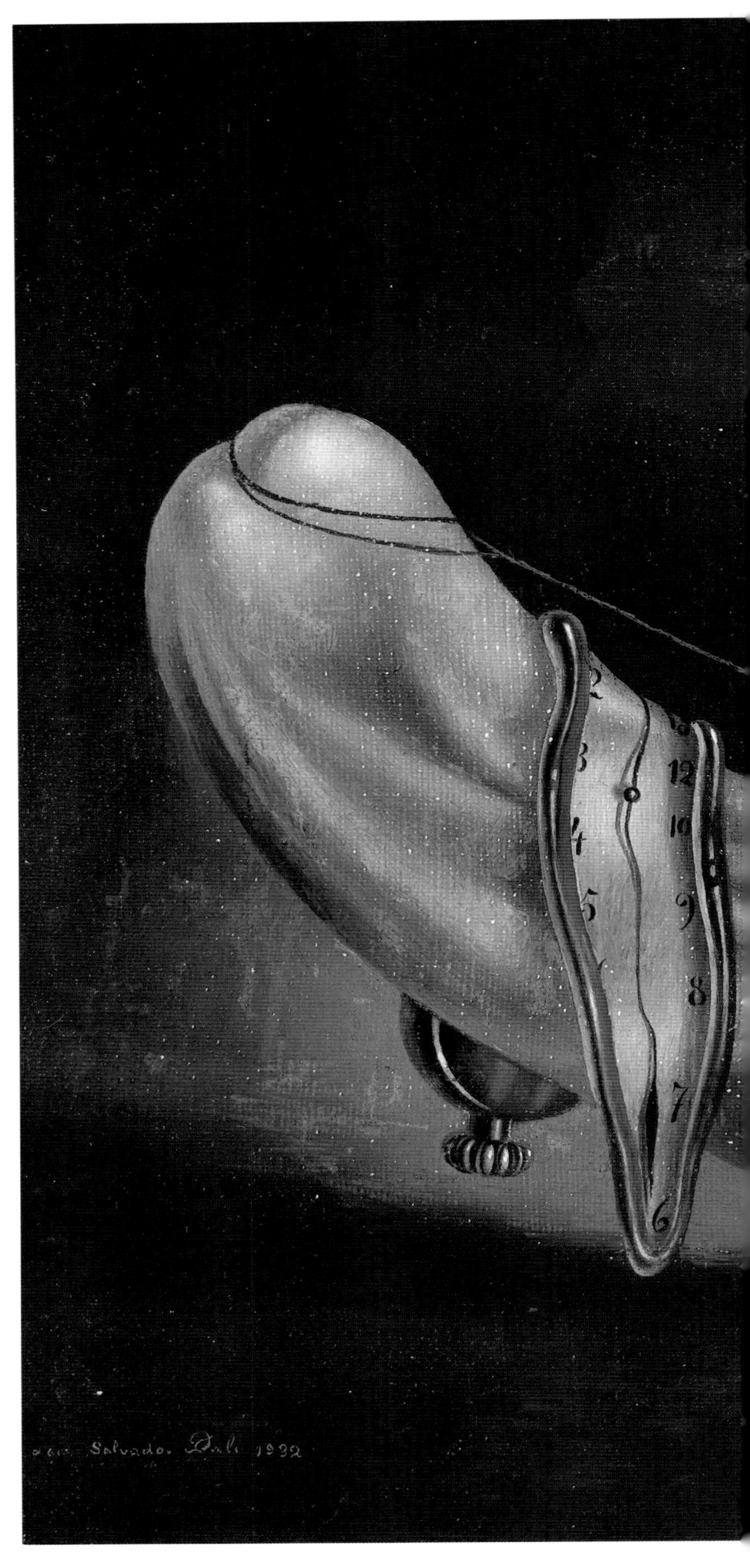

Catalan Bread 1932
Oil on canvas, $9\frac{9}{16} \times 13$ inches (24.13×33 cm)
Collection of The Salvador Dalí Museum, St. Petersburg, Florida

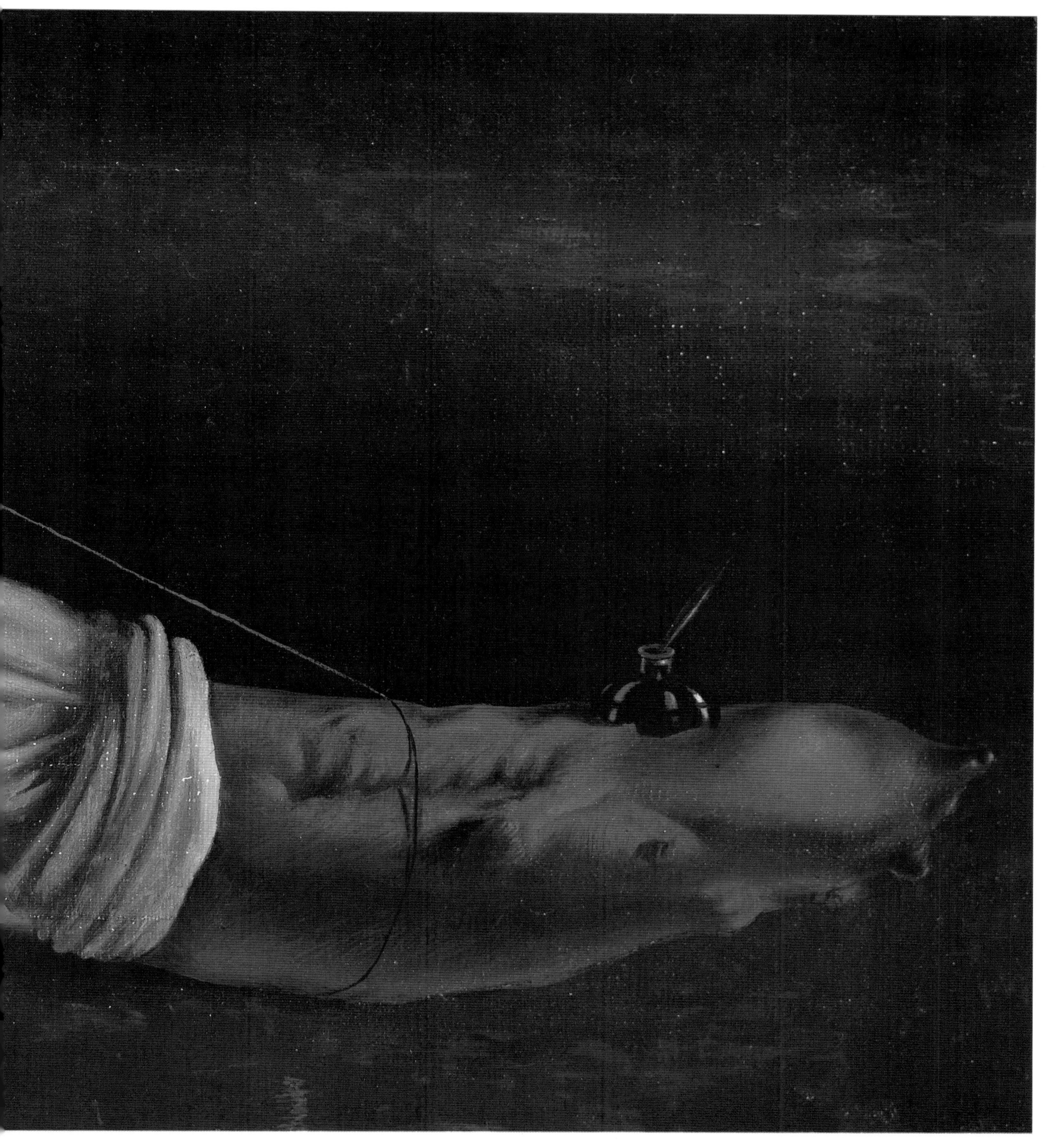

Accommodations of Desire 1929
Oil and collage on panel, 8⅝×13¾ inches (21.6×35 cm)
Private collection

LEFT
Le Spectre et le Fantôme *c.* 1931
Oil on canvas, 39.4×28.8 inches (100×73 cm)
Christie's, London

ABOVE
The Architectural Angelus of Millet 1933
Oil on canvas, 24¾×24 inches (73×60 cm)
Fundación Reina Sofia, Madrid

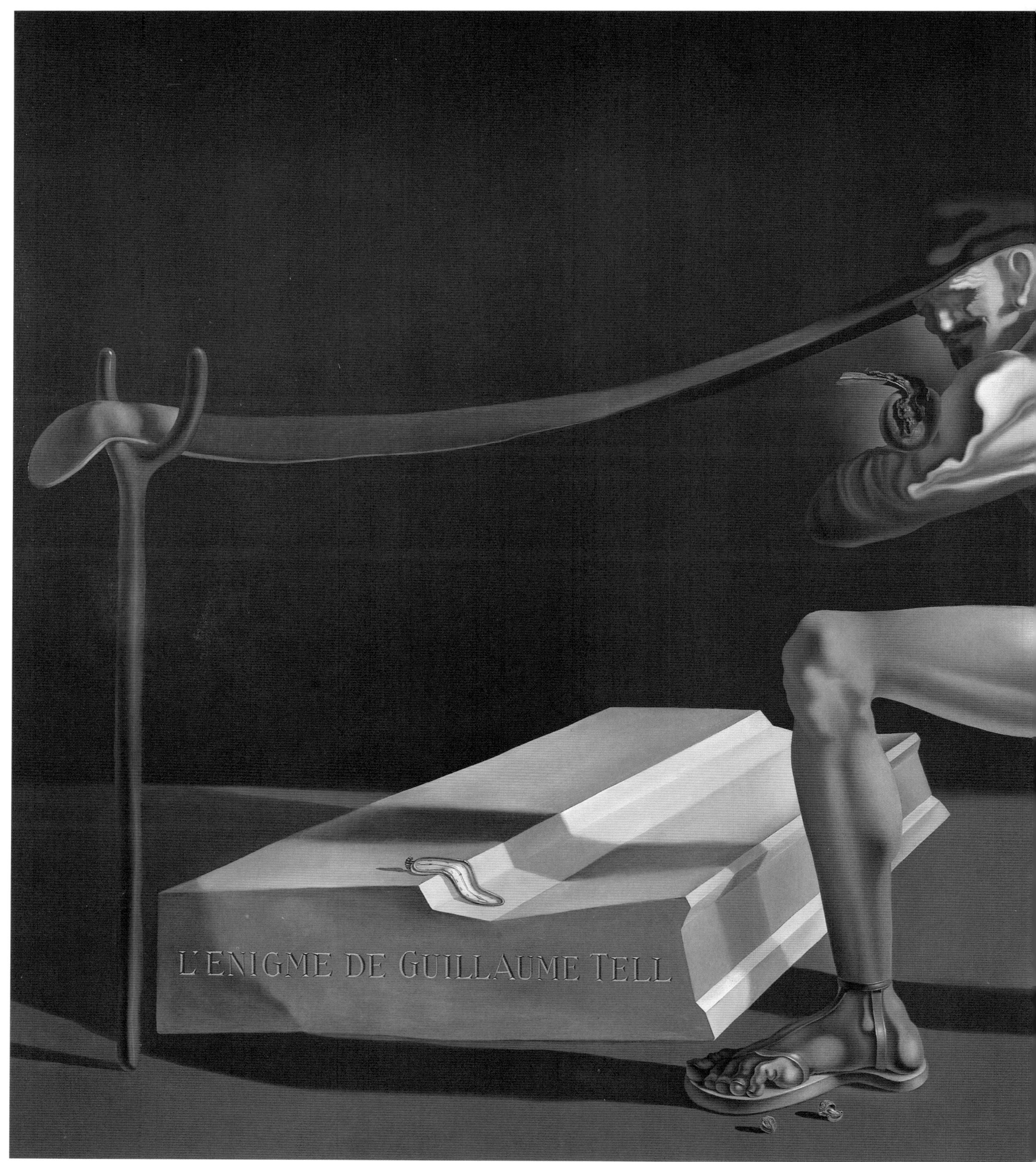

The Enigma of William Tell 1933
Oil on canvas, 79⅜×57½ inches (201.9×146 cm)
Statens Konstmuseer, Moderna Museet, Stockholm

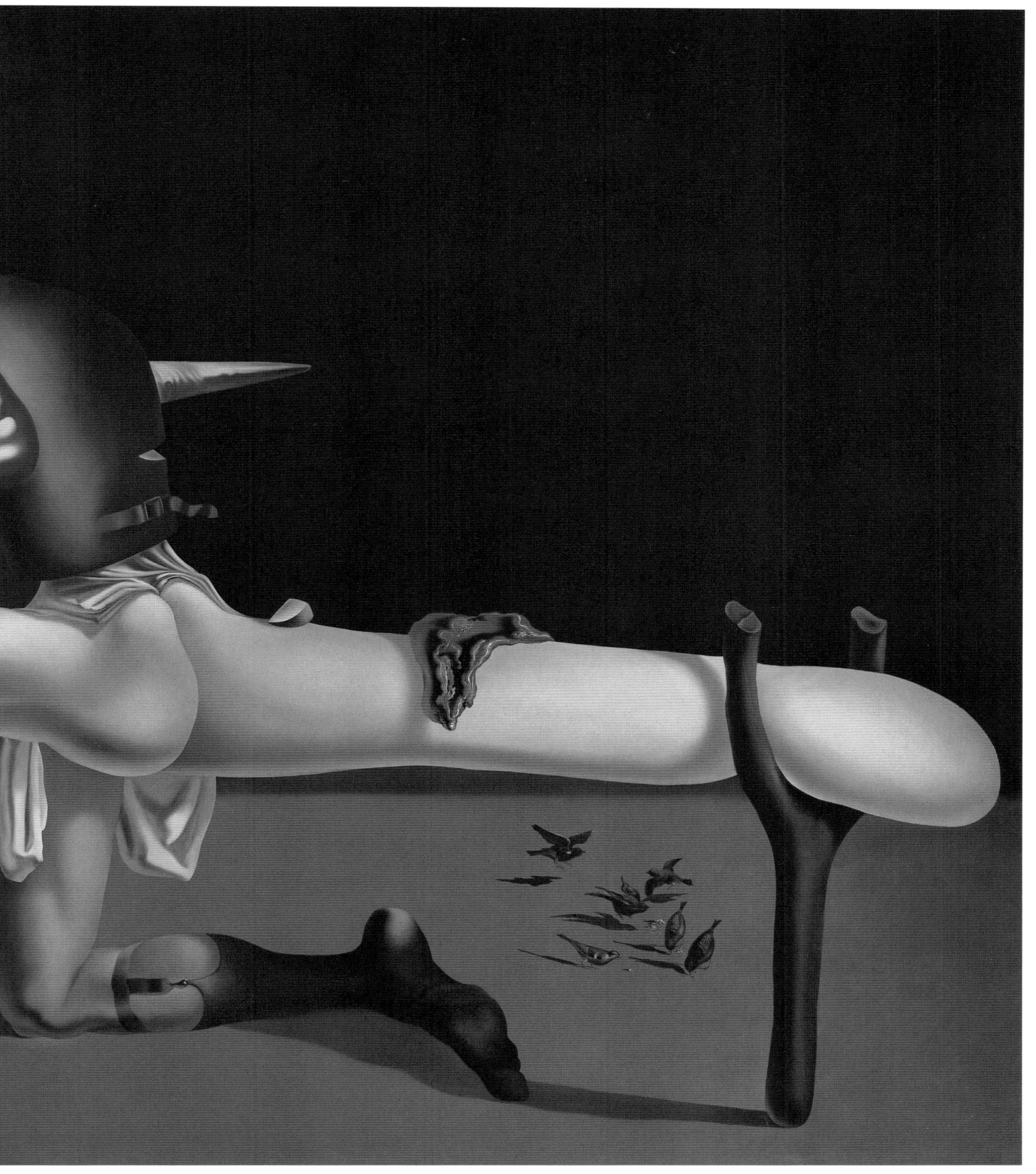

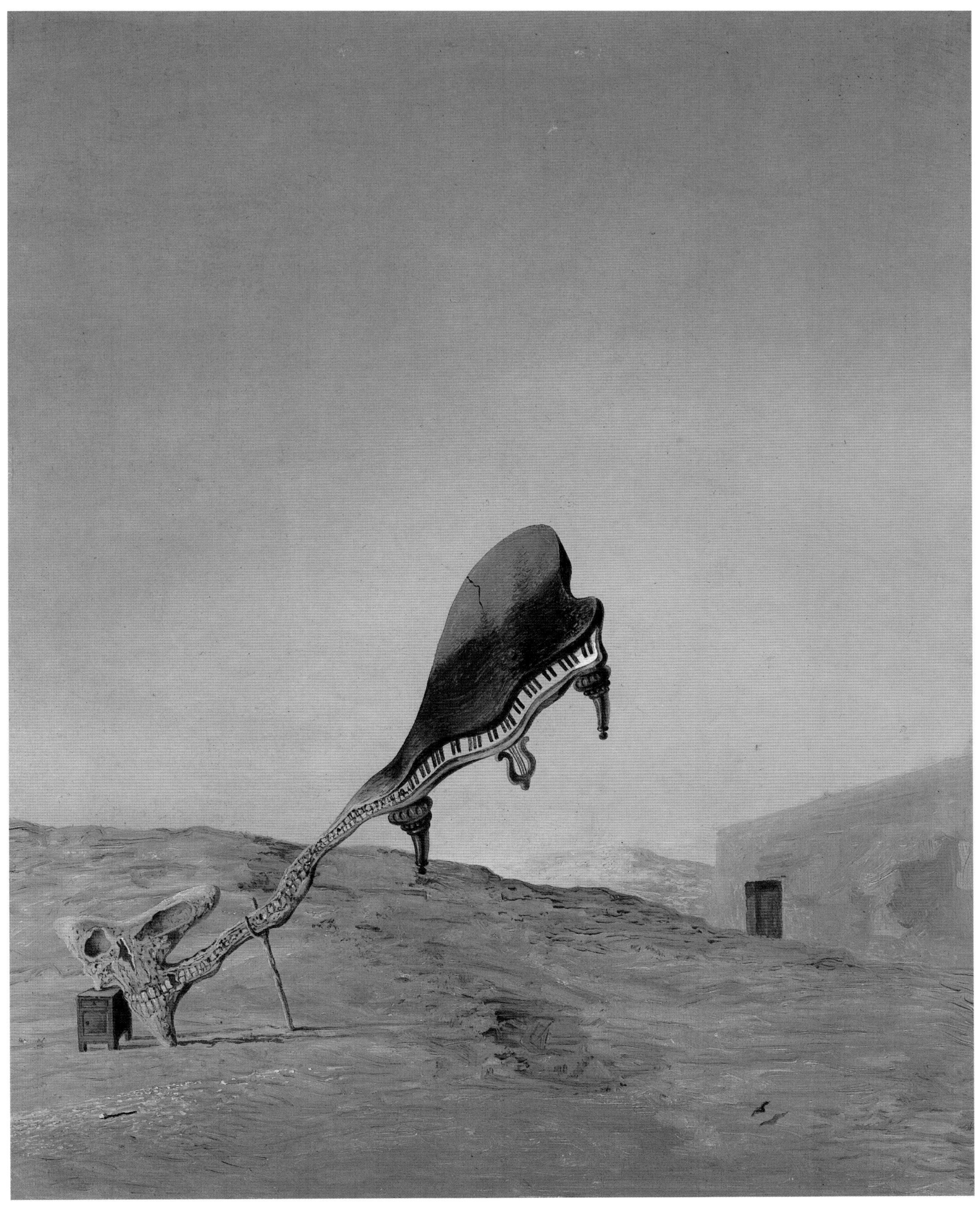

LEFT
Average Atmospherocephalic Bureaucrat in the Act of Milking a Cranial Harp 1933
Oil on canvas, 8¾×6½ inches (22×16.5 cm)
Collection of Mr and Mrs A. Reynolds Morse,
on loan to The Salvador Dalí Museum, St. Petersburg, Florida

ABOVE
Skull with its Lyric Appendage Leaning on a Night Table Which Should Have the Exact Temperature of a Cardinal Bird's Nest 1934
Oil on panel, 9½×7½ inches (24×19 cm)
Collection of Mr and Mrs A. Reynolds Morse,
on loan to The Salvador Dalí Museum, St. Petersburg, Florida

ABOVE
The Ghost of Vermeer of Delft Which can be Used as a Table 1934
Oil on canvas, 7⅛×5½ inches (18.1×14 cm)
Collection of Mr and Mrs A. Reynolds Morse, on loan to The Salvador Dalí Museum, St. Petersburg, Florida

LEFT
Meditation on the Harp 1932-34
Oil on canvas, 26¼×18½ inches (66.7×47 cm)
Collection of The Salvador Dalí Museum, St. Petersburg, Florida

The Weaning of Furniture-Nutrition 1934
Oil on panel, 9½×7½ inches (24×19 cm)
Collection of Mr and Mrs A. Reynolds Morse,
on loan to The Salvador Dalí Museum, St. Petersburg, Florida

Archaeological Reminiscence of Millet's Angelus 1933-35,
Oil on panel, 12½×15½ inches (31.8×39.4 cm)
Collection of The Salvador Dalí Museum, St. Petersburg, Florida

Atmospheric Skull Sodomizing a Grand Piano 1934
Oil on panel, 5½×7 inches (14×17.8 cm)
Collection of Mr and Mrs A. Reynolds Morse, on loan to The Salvador Dalí Museum, St. Petersburg, Florida

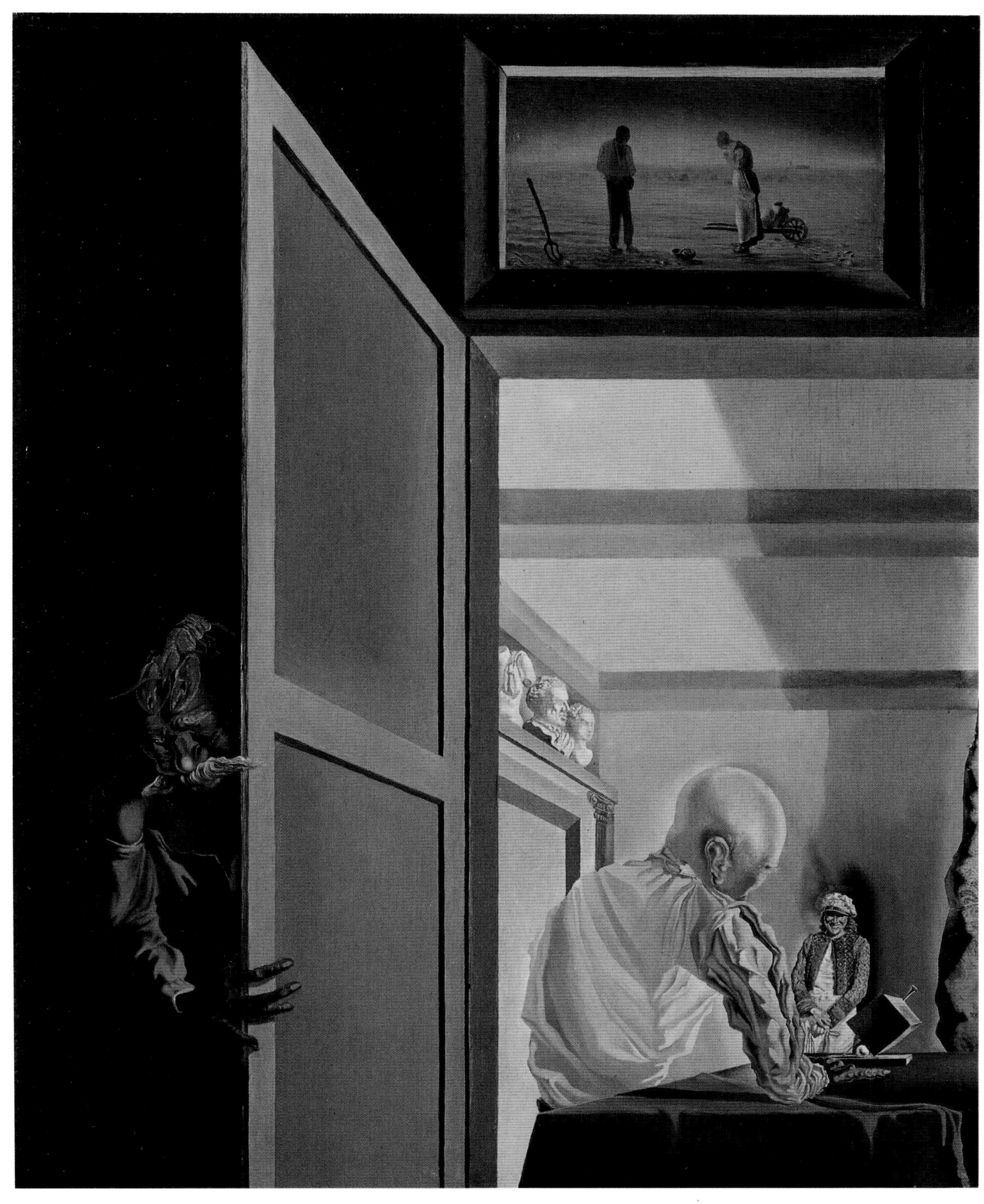

ABOVE
Gala and the Angelus of Millet Immediately Preceding the Arrival of the Conic Anamorphoses 1933
Oil on panel, 9 7/16 × 7 3/8 inches (24.1 × 18.8 cm)
National Gallery of Canada, Ottowa

LEFT
Mae West *c.*1934
Gouache over photographic print, 11 1/8 × 7 inches (28.3 × 17.8 cm)
Gift of Mrs Gilbert W. Chapman in memory of Charles B. Goodspeed, 1949, The Art Institute of Chicago

Paranoiac-Critical Solitude 1935
Oil on panel, 7½×9⁹⁄₁₆ inches (19×22.9 cm)
Former collection of the Edward James Foundation, Sussex, now private collection

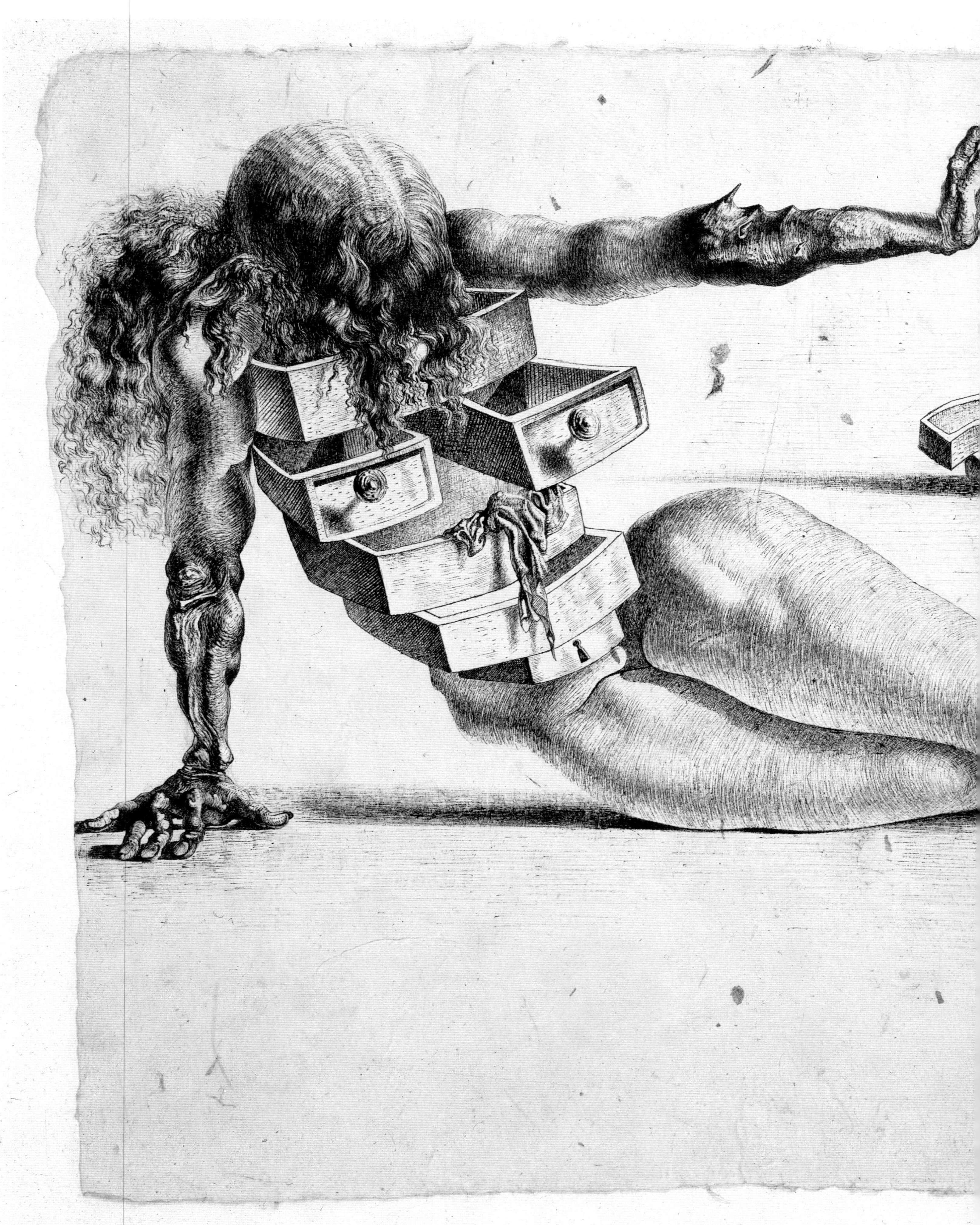

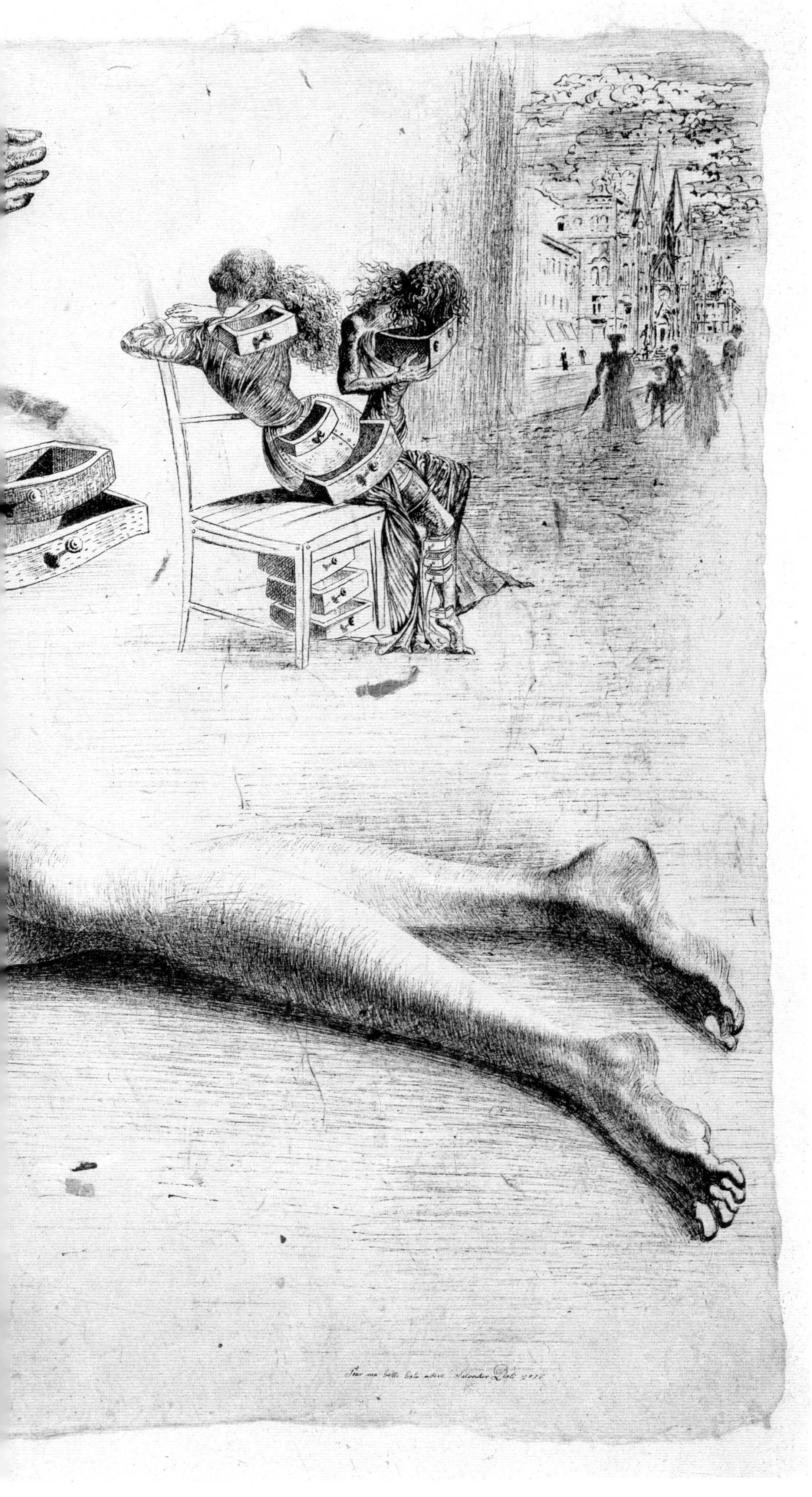
Salvador Dalí

ABOVE AND RIGHT (DETAIL)
Soft Construction with Boiled Beans – Premonition of Civil War *c.*1936
Oil on canvas, 29 5/16×39 3/8 inches (74.4×100 cm)
Philadelphia Museum of Art: Louise and Walter Arensberg Collection

PRECEDING PAGES
City of Drawers 1936
Indian ink on paper, 12.6×16.3 inches (32×41.5 cm)
Former collection of the Edward James Foundation, Sussex, now private collection

Suburbs of a Paranoiac-Critical Town: Afternoon on the Outskirts of European History 1936
Oil on panel, 18½×26 inches (47×66 cm)
Former collection of the Edward James Foundation, Sussex, now private collection

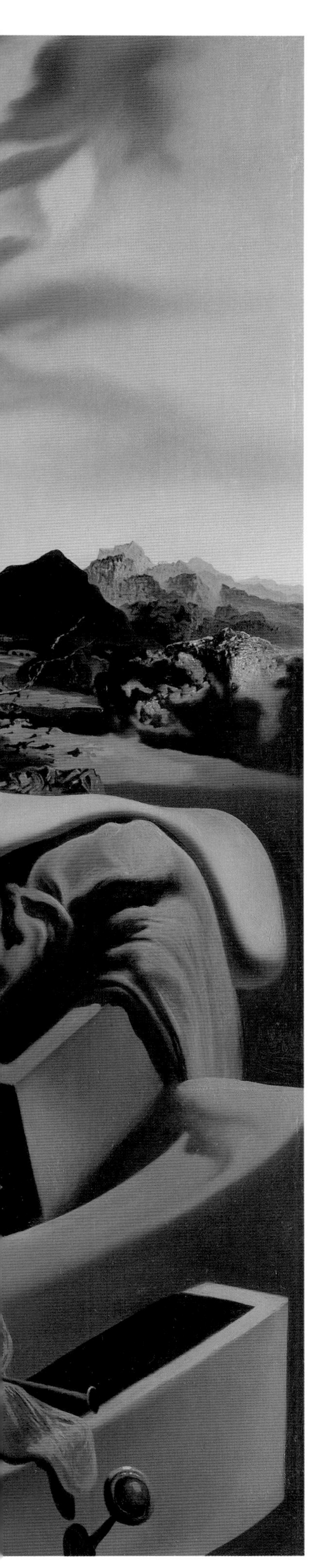

Autumn Cannibalism 1936
Oil on canvas, 25⅝×25⅝ inches (65.3×65.3 cm)
Tate Gallery, London

The Enigma of Hitler 1937
Oil on panel, 39⅜×59 inches (100×150 cm)
Private collection

Metamorphosis of Narcissus 1937
Oil on canvas, 20⅛×30¾ inches (51.3×78 cm)
Tate Gallery, London

Swans Reflecting Elephants 1937
Oil on canvas, 20⅛×30⅜ inches (51.3×77.2 cm)
Former collection of the Edward James Foundation, Sussex, now private collection

Imperial Violets 1938
Oil on canvas, 39¼×56⅛ inches (99.5×142.5 cm)
Arango Collection, Madrid

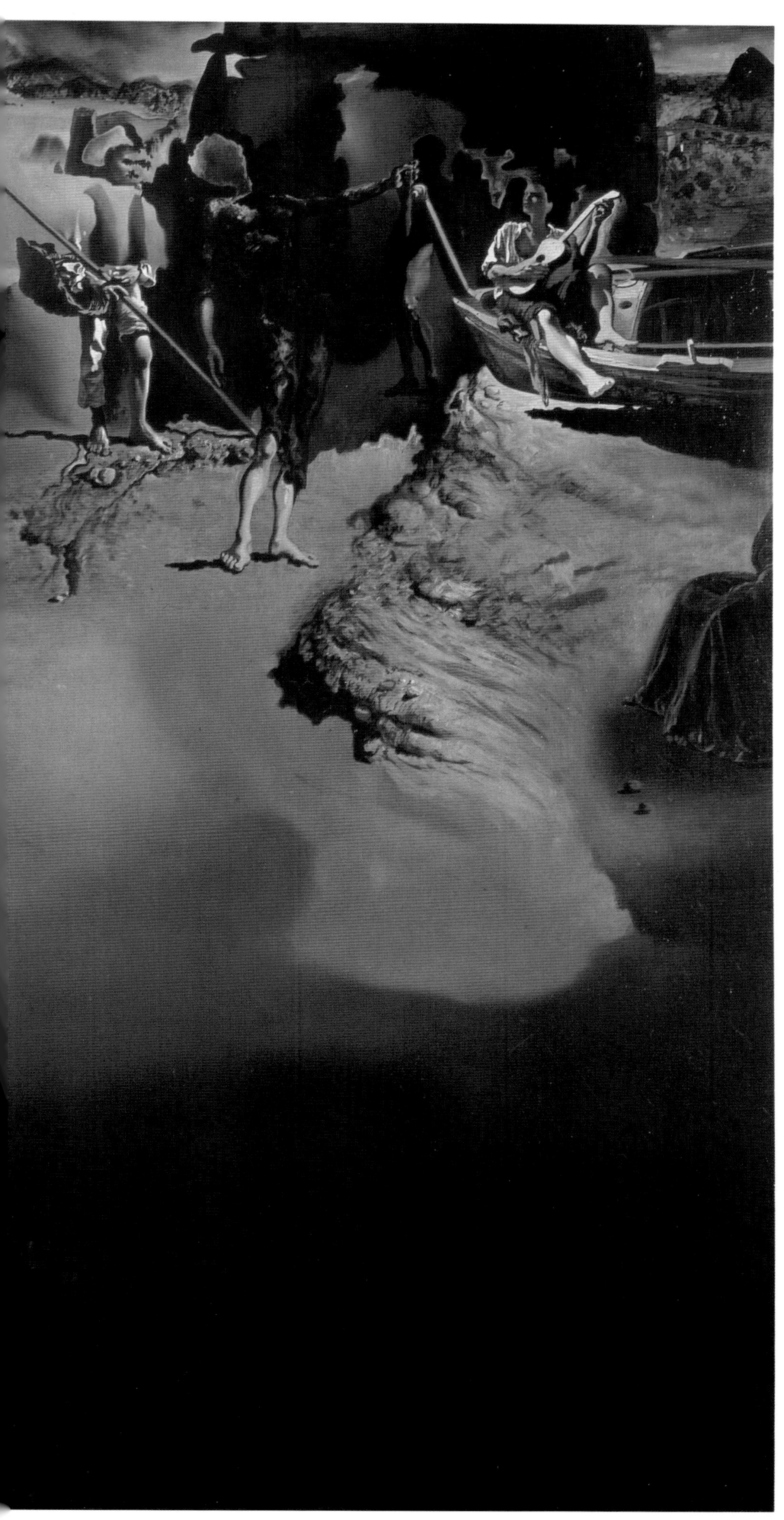

Impressions of Africa 1938
Oil on canvas,
36×46¼ inches (91.5×117.5 cm)
Boymans-van Beuningen Museum, Rotterdam

Beach Scene with Telephone 1938
Oil on canvas, 29×36¼ inches (74.2×92.8 cm)
Tate Gallery, London

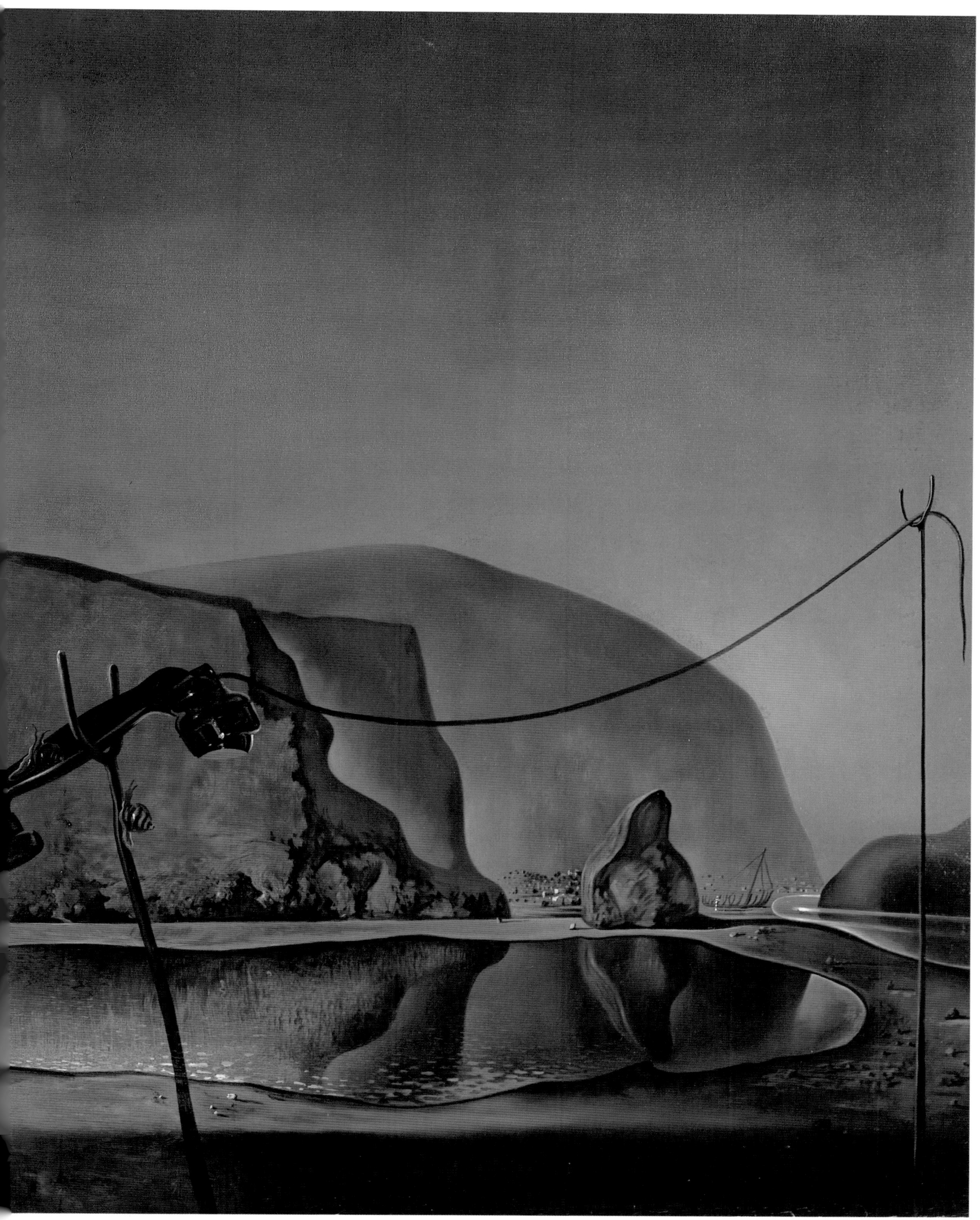

Slave Market with the Disappearing Bust of Voltaire 1940
Oil on canvas, 18¼×25⅜ inches (46.4×64.5 cm)
Collection of The Salvador Dalí Museum, St. Petersburg, Florida

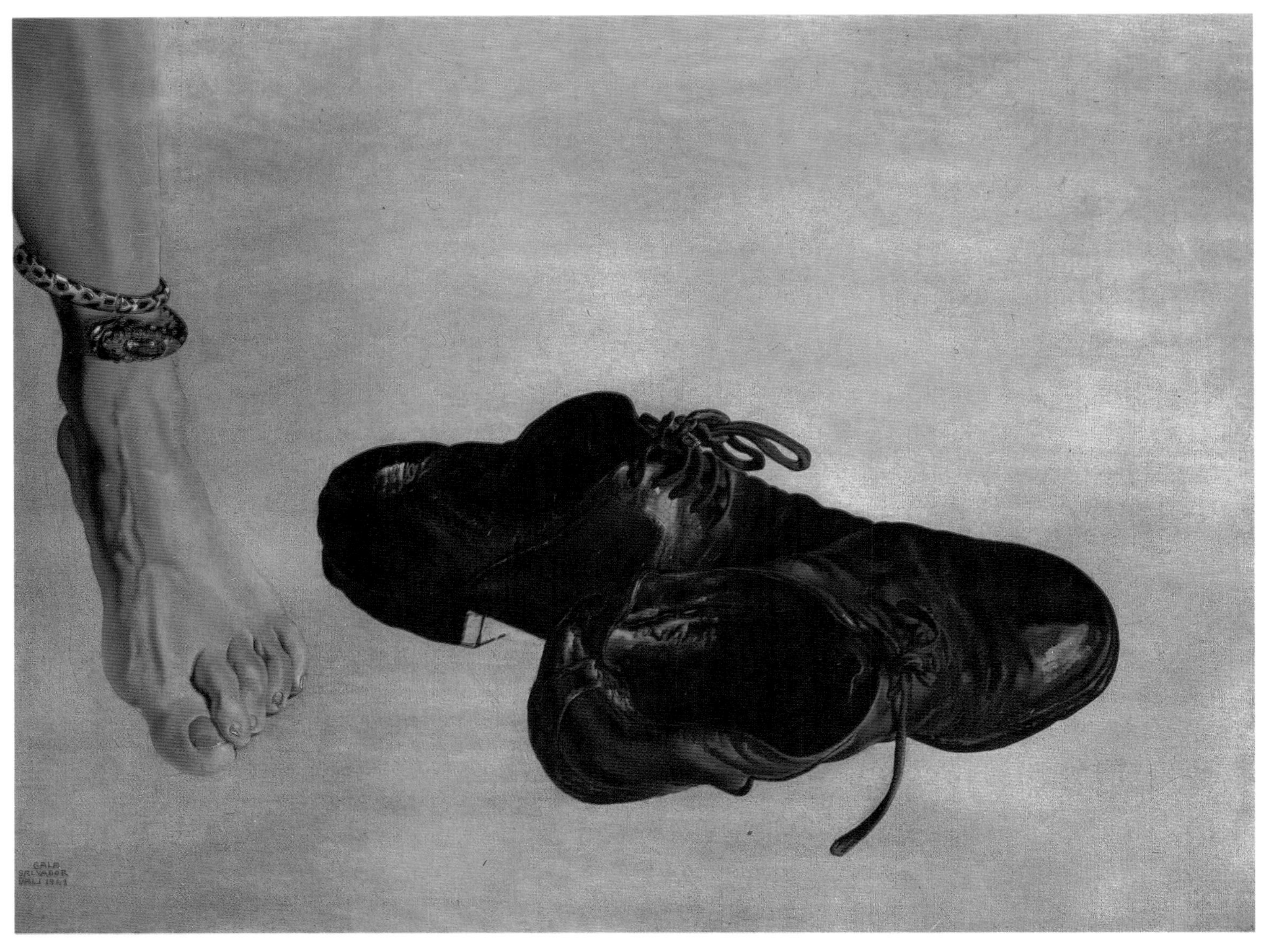

Original Sin 1941
Oil on canvas, 32×40 inches (81.3×101.6 cm)
Former collection of the Edward James Foundation, Sussex, now private collection

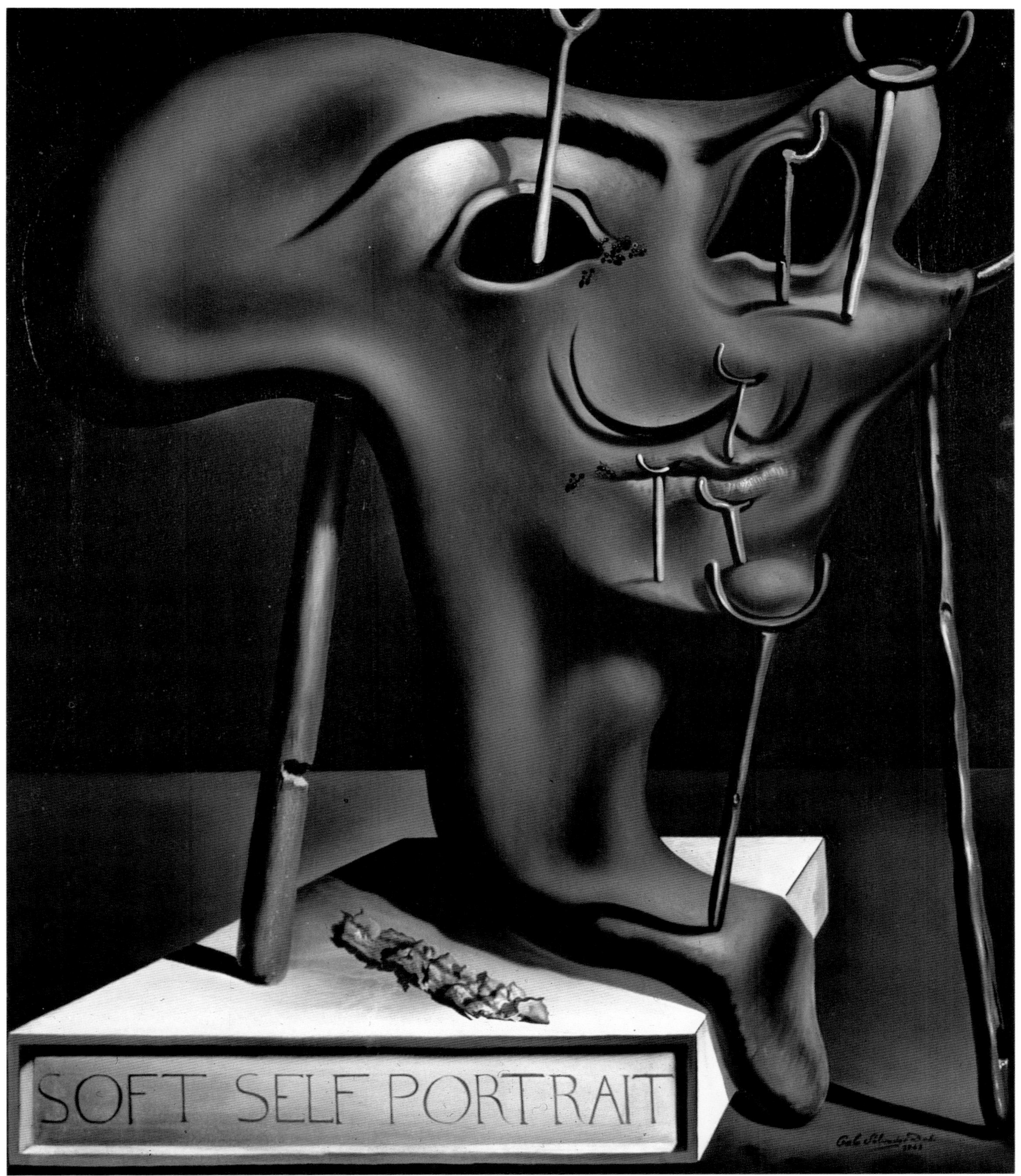

Soft Self-Portrait with a Rasher of Grilled Bacon 1941
Oil on canvas, 24×20 inches (61×50.8 cm)
Fundación Gala-Salvador-Dalí, Figueras

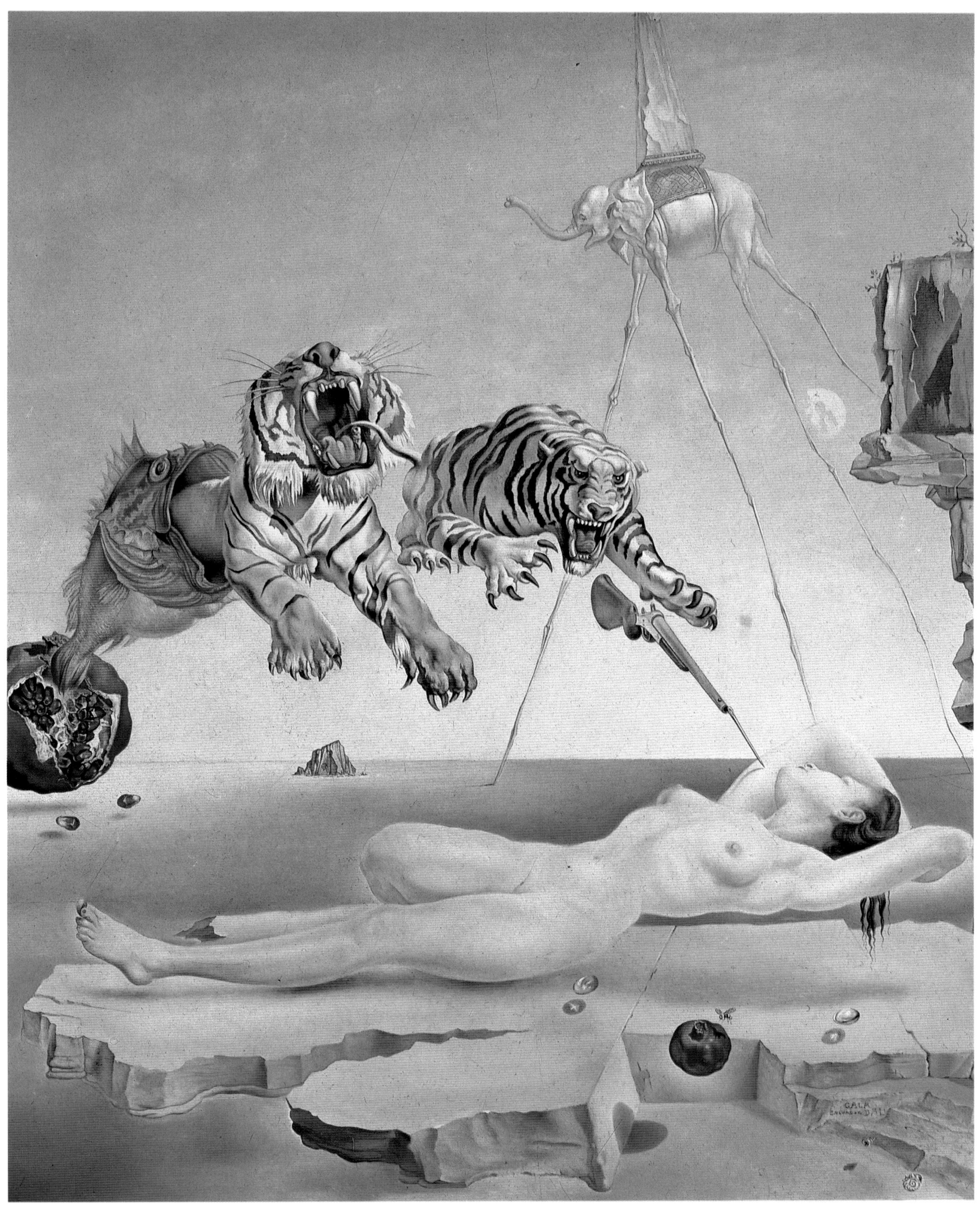

ABOVE
One Second Before Awakening from a Dream Caused by the Flight of a Bee Around a Pomegranate 1944
Oil on canvas, 8¼×16⅛ inches (51×41 cm)
Private collection, Lugano

LEFT
The Poetry of America 1943
Oil on canvas, 46×31 inches (117×79 cm)
Fundación Gala-Salvador-Dalí, Figueras

Geopoliticus Child Watching the Birth of the New Man 1943
Oil on canvas, 18×20½ inches (45.7×52 cm)
Collection of The Salvador Dalí Museum, St. Petersburg, Florida

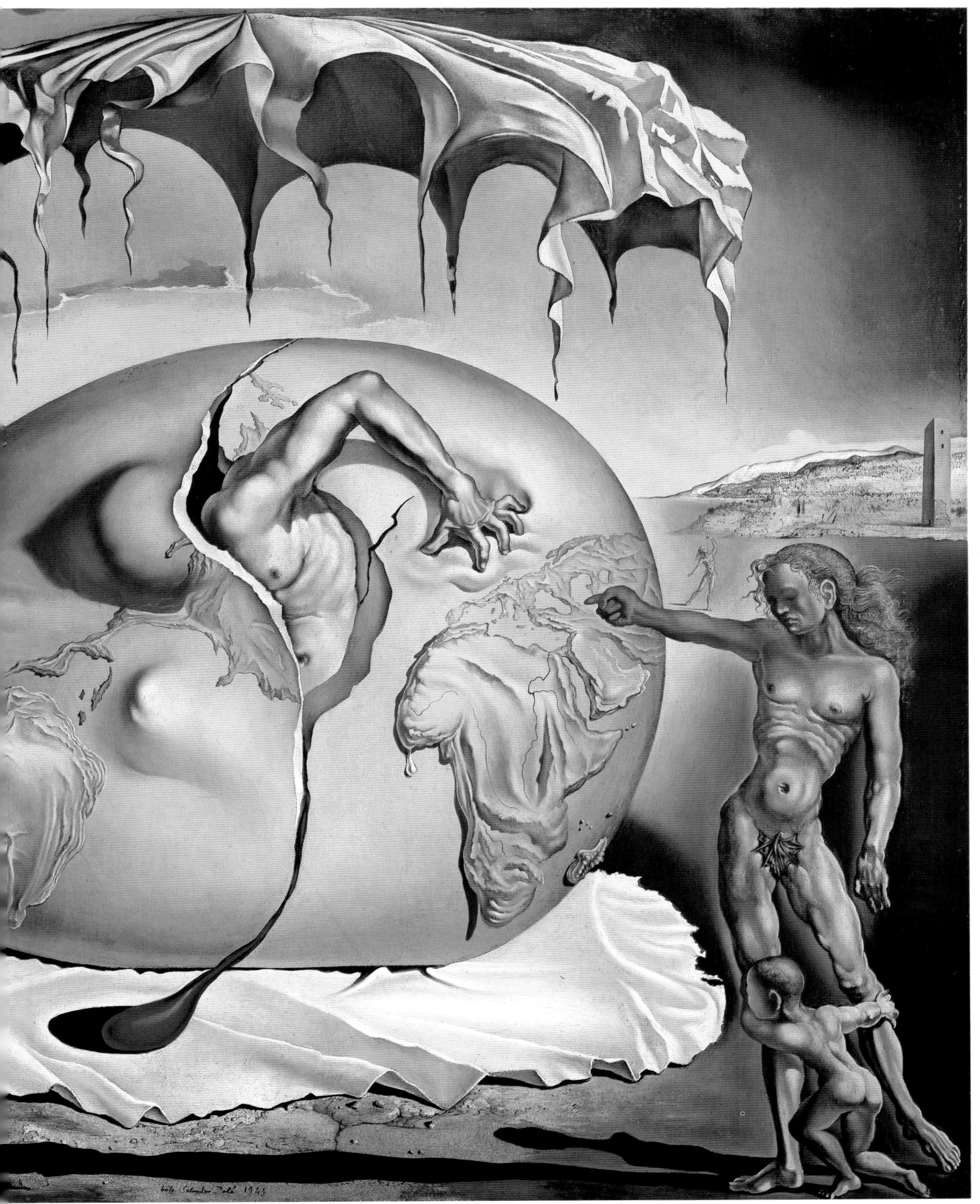

Portrait of Frau Isabel Styler-Tas 1945
Oil on canvas, 25¾×33⅞ inches (65.5×86 cm)
Staatliche Museen zu Berlin, Preussischer Kulturbesitz, Nationalgalerie

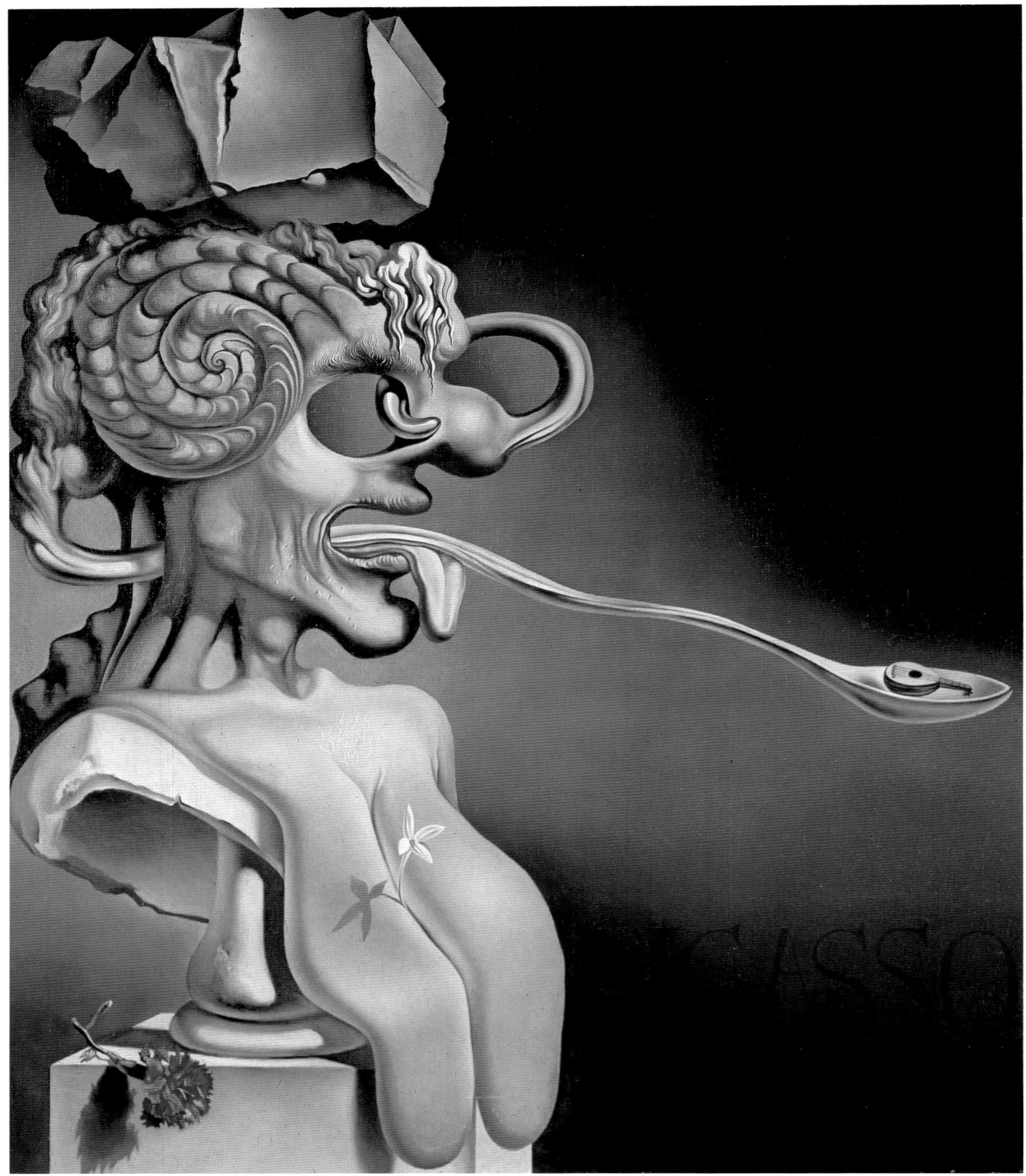

ABOVE
Portrait of Picasso 1947
Oil on canvas, $25\frac{1}{4}\times21\frac{1}{2}$ *inches (64.2×54.6 cm)*
Fundación Gala-Salvador-Dalí, Figueras

RIGHT
First Study for the Madonna of Port Lligat 1949
Oil on canvas, 19.3×14.8 inches (48.9×37.5 cm)
Marquette University Fine Art Committee, Milwaukee, Wisconsin

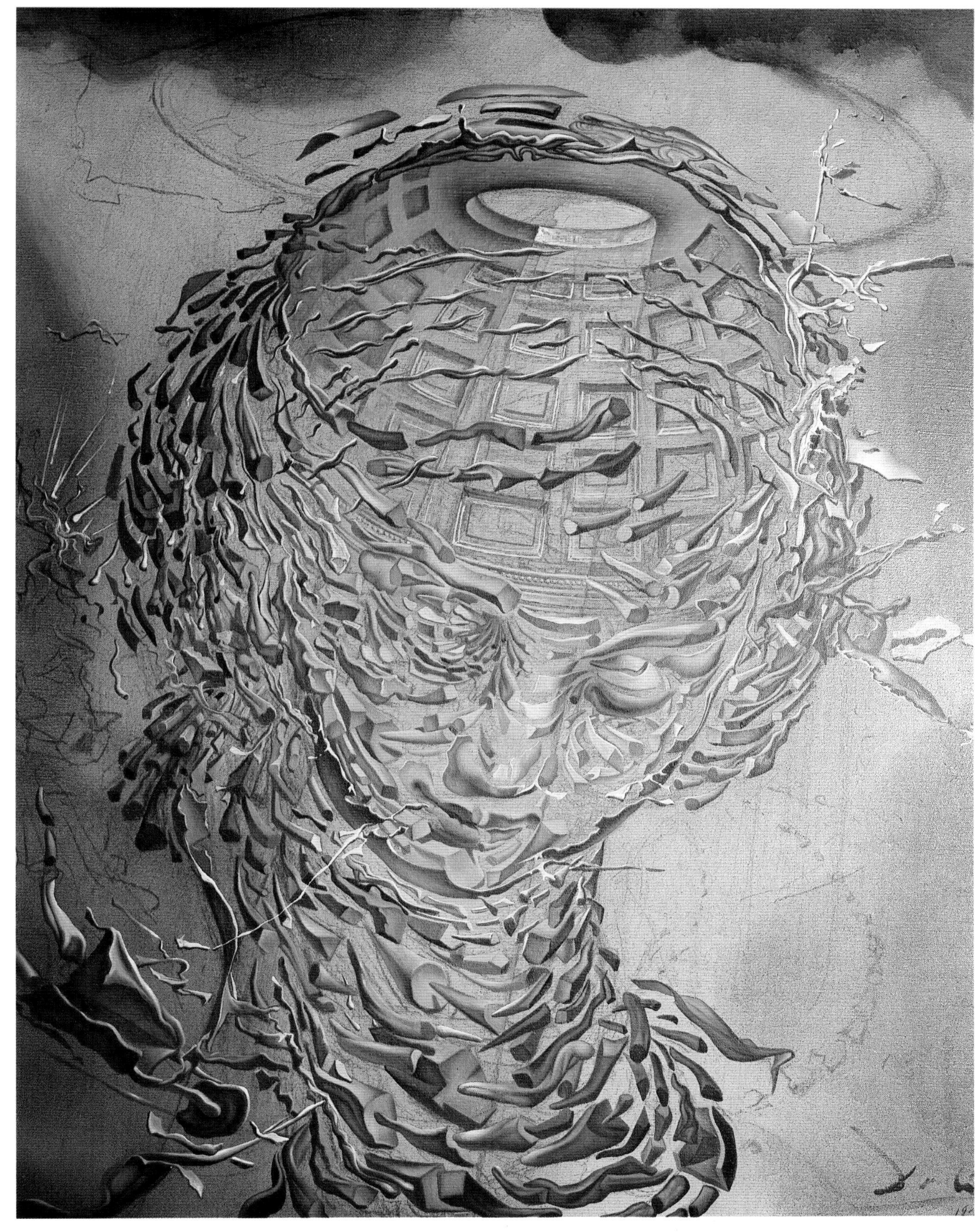

ABOVE
Raphaelesque Head Exploding 1951
Oil on canvas, 16⅞×13 inches (43×33.3 cm)
Private collection, on loan to the Scottish National Gallery of Modern Art, Edinburgh

LEFT
Atomic Leda 1949
Oil on canvas, 24×17¾ inches (61.1×45.3 cm)
Fundación Gala-Salvador-Dalí, Figueras

ABOVE

The Skull of Zurbarán 1956

Oil on canvas, 39½×39½ inches (100.3×100.3 cm)

Hirshhorn Museum and Sculpture Garden, Smithsonian Institution. Gift of the Joseph H. Hirshhorn Foundation, 1966

LEFT

Corpus Hypercubicus 1954

Oil on canvas, 76⅜×48⅞ inches (195.6×125.2 cm)

Metropolitan Museum of Art, New York

Rhinocerotic Figure of Phidias' Illisos 1954
Oil on canvas, 40×51½ inches (101.5×131 cm)
Private collection

The Sacrament of the Last Supper 1955
Oil on canvas, 65⅝×105½ inches (166.7×267 cm)
National Gallery of Art, Washington, Chester Dale Collection

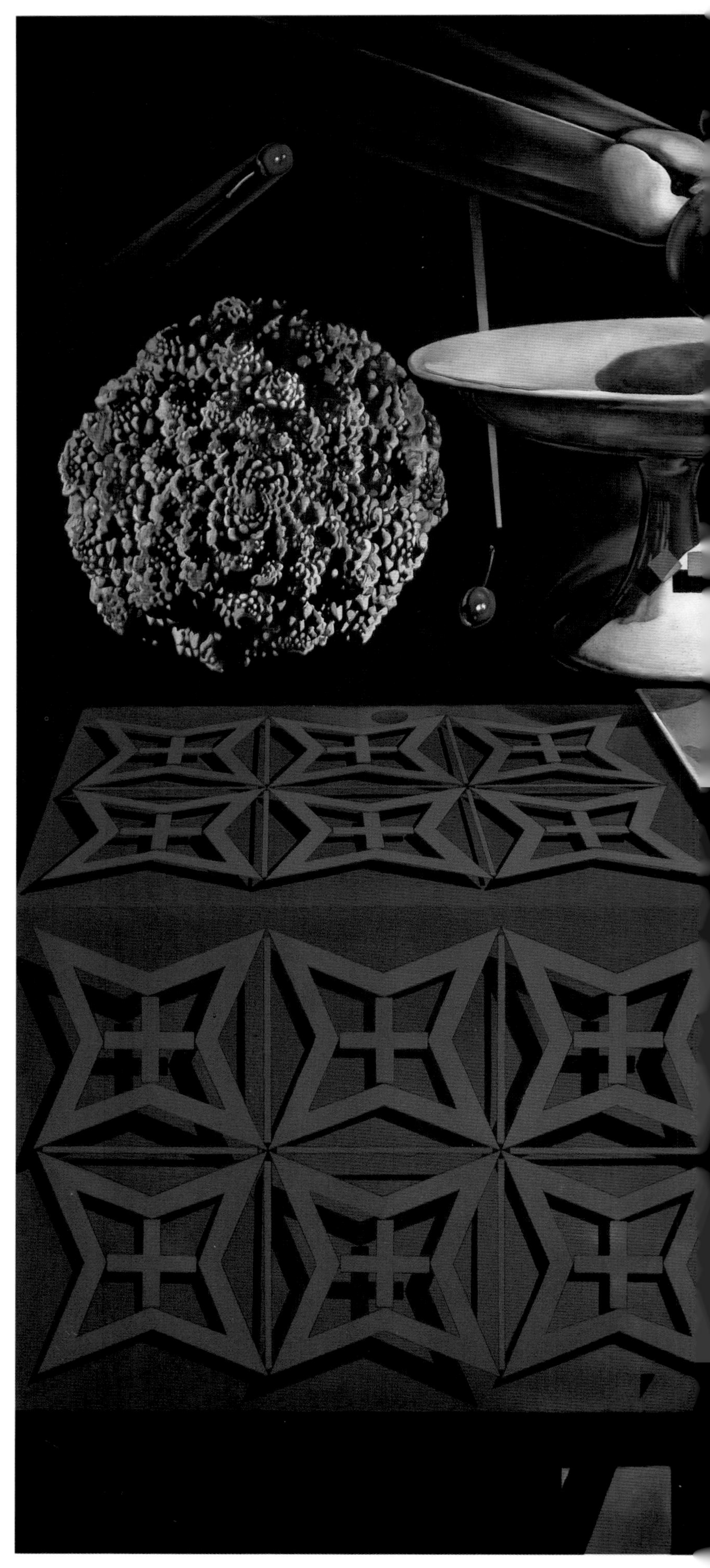

Nature Morte Vivante (Animated Still Life) 1956
Oil on canvas, 49¼×63 inches (125×160 cm)
Collection of The Salvador Dalí Museum,
St. Petersburg, Florida

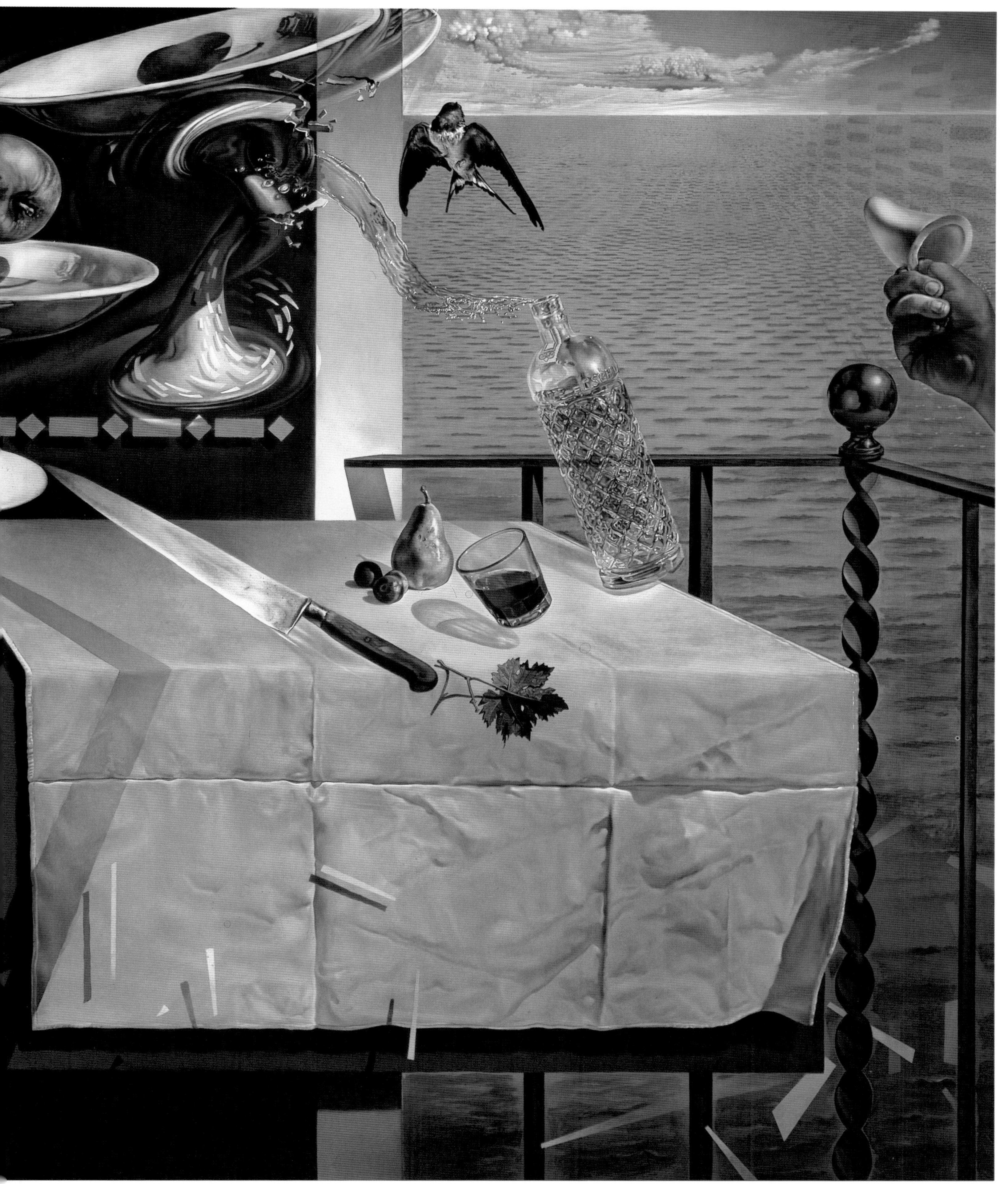

LEFT AND ABOVE (DETAIL)
Velázquez Painting the Infanta Margarita with the Lights and Shadows of His Own Glory 1958
Oil on canvas, 60½×36¼ inches (153.7×92.1 cm)
Collection of The Salvador Dalí Museum,
St. Petersburg, Florida

ABOVE

Dalí's Hand Drawing Back the Golden Fleece in the Form of a Cloud to Show Gala the Dawn, Completely Nude, Very Very Far Away Behind the Sun 1977

Oil on canvas, stereoscopic work in two parts, each 23⅝×23⅝ inches (64.9×64.9 cm)

Spanish State Patrimony

LEFT

The Discovery of America by Christopher Columbus 1958-59

Oil on canvas, 161½×122⅛ inches (410.2×310.2 cm)

Collection of The Salvador Dalí Museum, St. Petersburg, Florida

Tunny Fishing 1966-67
Oil on canvas, 157½×118⅛ inches (400×300 cm)
Paul Richard Foundation, Bandol, France

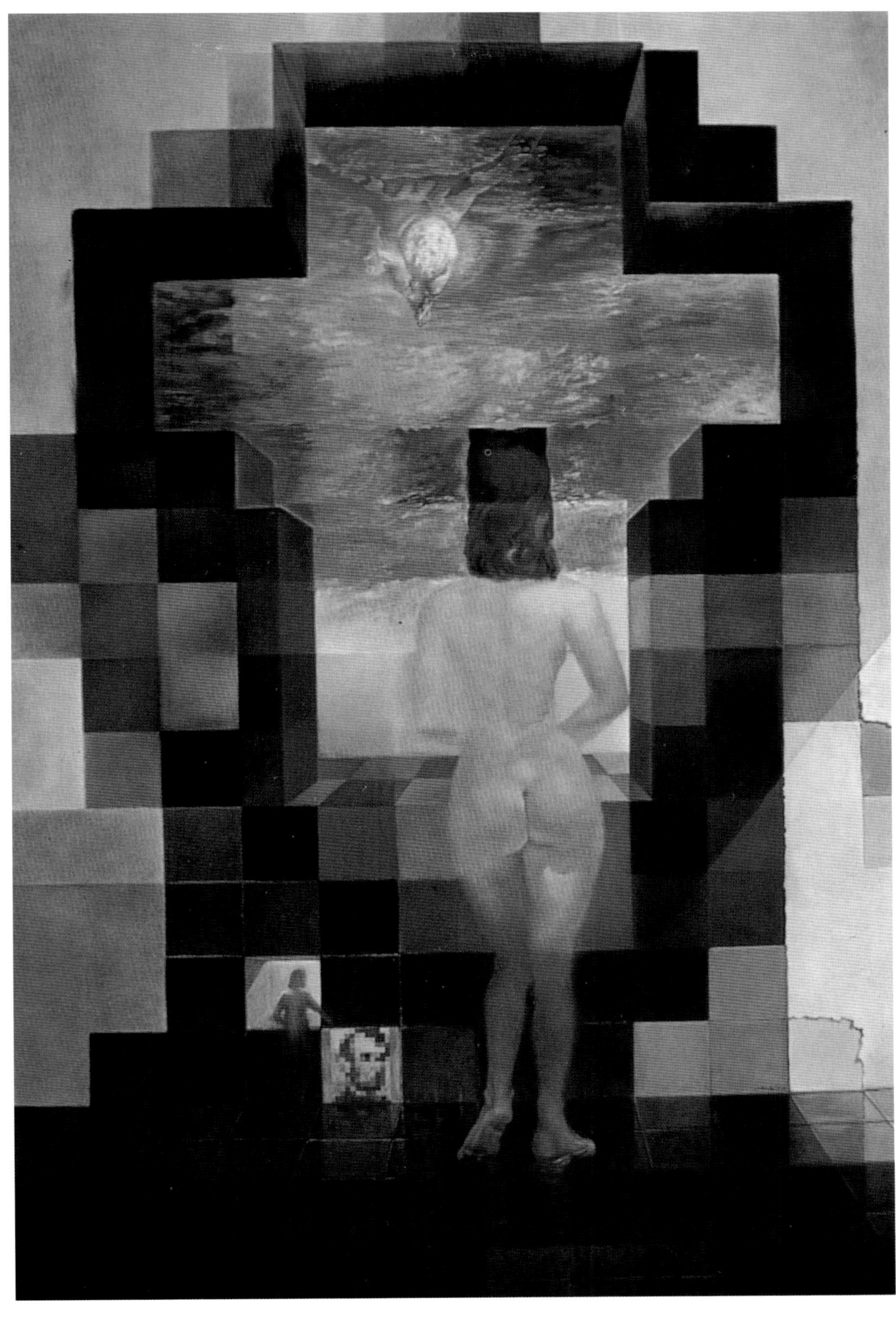

LEFT
The Hallucinogenic Toreador 1969-70
Oil on canvas, 157×119 inches (398.7×302.3 cm)
Collection of The Salvador Dalí Museum,
St. Petersburg, Florida

ABOVE
Gala Contemplating the Mediterranean Sea Which at Twenty Meters Becomes the Portrait of Abraham Lincoln (Homage to Rothko) 1976
Oil on canvas, 99¼×75½ inches (254.1×193.3 cm)
Fundación Gala-Salvador-Dalí, Figueras

Dawn, Noon, Sunset and Twilight 1979
Oil on wood, 96×48 inches (244×122 cm)
Fundación Gala-Salvador-Dalí, Figueras

ACKNOWLEDGMENTS

The publisher would like to thank Martin Bristow, the designer; Suzanne O'Farrell, the picture researcher; Clare Haworth-Maden, the editor; Veronica Price and Nicki Giles, for production; and the museums, agencies and individuals listed below for supplying the illustrations.

Arango Collection, Madrid/ARXIU MAS: page 90

ARXIU MAS: pages 15 (bottom), 18 (top), 23 (top)/former Edward James Foundation, Sussex, now private collection: page 97

Bridgeman Art Library/Boymans-van Beuningen Museum, Rotterdam, page 92/Christie's, London: pages 40, 58/ Marquette University, Fine Art Committee, Milwaukee, Wisconsin: page 107//Private collection: page 48/former Edward James Foundation, Sussex, now private collection: pages 56, 74, 76, 80, 88

British Film Institute, London: page 8 (top)

© 1992 The Art Institute of Chicago, All Rights Reserved, Gift of Mrs Gilbert W. Chapman in memory of Charles B. Goodspeed, 1949: page 72

Copyright, 1936 *Time* Inc.: page 12

Collection of The Salvador Dalí Museum, St. Petersburg, Florida, photograph copyright 1993 Salvador Dalí Museum, Inc.: pages 32, 38, 54, 64, 68, 96, 102, 116, 118, 119, 121, 124

Fundación Gala-Salvador-Dalí, Figueras/ARXIU MAS: pages 1, 97, 100, 106, 108, 125, 126

Peggy Guggenheim Collection, Venice. Photographer: David Heald, photograph © 1991 The Solomon R. Guggenheim Foundation: page 52

Hirshhorn Museum and Sculpture Garden, Smithsonian Institute, Gift of the Joseph H. Hirshhorn Foundation, 1966/ ARXIU MAS: page 111

Hulton-Deutsch Collection: pages 6, 8 (bottom), 9 (bottom)

Metropolitan Museum of Art, New York/ARXIU MAS: page 110

Collection of Mr and Mrs A. Reynolds Morse, on loan to The Salvador Dalí Museum, St. Petersburg, Florida, photograph copyright 1993 Salvador Dalí Museum, Inc.: pages 35, 46, 50, 62, 63, 65, 70/ARXIU MAS: page 66

Musée D'Orsay, © Photo Réunion des Musées Nationaux: page 15 (top)

Museo Arte Moderno, Barcelona/ARXIU MAS: page 13

Museo Arte Moderno, Madrid/ARXIU MAS: page 31

Museo Español Arte Contemperáneo, Madrid/ARXIU MAS: pages 28, 30, 34

National Gallery of Art, Washington, Chester Dale Collection: page 114

National Gallery of Canada, Ottawa: page 73

Palacio Zarzuela, Madrid/ARXIU MAS: page 14

Philadelphia Museum of Art: Louise and Walter Arensberg Collection: page 78

Pictorial Press: page 7

Photo Philippe Migeat/© Centre G. Pompidou, Paris: page 36

Popperfoto: page 20

Private collection: page 56

Private collection/ARXIU MAS: pages 84, 112

Private collection, Barcelona/ARXIU MAS: page 29

Private collection, Madrid/ARXIU MAS: pages 11, 21, 23 (bottom)

Private collection, New York/ARXIU MAS: page 42

Private collection, Santander/ARXIU MAS: page 18 (bottom)

Private collection, on loan to the Scottish National Gallery of Modern Art, Edinburgh: page 109

Paul Richard Foundation, Bandol, France/ARXIU MAS: page 122

Royal Palace, Madrid/ARXIU MAS: page 24

Fundación Reina Sofia, Madrid/ARXIU MAS: page 59

Spanish State Patrimony/ARXIU MAS: pages 26, 27, 43, 44/ Beatrice Hata: page 120

Staatliche Museen zu Berlin, Preussischer Kulturbesitz, Nationalgalerie, photo: Jörg P. Anders, Berlin: page 104

Statens Konstmuseer, Moderna Museet, Stockholm: page 60

Tate Gallery, London: pages 2, 82, 86, 94

Courtesy of the Trustees of the Victoria and Albert Museum, London: page 25

Wadsworth Atheneum, Hartford, Ella Gallup Sumner and Mary Catlin Sumner Collection: page 4

Weidenfeld Archive/Museum of Art and History of Saint-Denis: pages 9 (top), 10/Courtesy Wadsworth Atheneum: page 17